Information Assurance

Trends in Vulnerabilities, Threats, and Technologies

Information Assurance

Trends in Vulnerabilities, Threats, and Technologies

edited by Jacques S. Gansler and
Hans Binnendijk

NATIONAL DEFENSE UNIVERSITY
CENTER FOR TECHNOLOGY AND NATIONAL SECURITY POLICY
WASHINGTON, D.C.
2004

ISBN 1-57906-069-2
First Printing, January 2005

NDU CTNSP publications are sold by the U.S. Government Printing Office. For ordering information, call (202) 512-1800 or write to the Superintendant of Documents, U.S. Government Printing Office, Washington, D.C. 20402. For GPO publications on-line access their Website at: http://www.access.gpo.gov/su_docs/sale.html.

For current publications of the Center for Technology and National Security Policy, consult the National Defense University Website at: http://www.ndu.edu/ctnsp/publications.html.

Contents

Information Assurance

Trends in Vulnerabilities, Threats, and Technologies

Introduction

Jacques S. Gansler and Hans Binnendijk

One of the missions of the Center for Technology and National Security Policy at National Defense University is to study the transformation of America's military and to explore the consequences of the information revolution. To further this mission, National Defense University, in collaboration with The Center for Public Policy and Private Enterprise of the University of Maryland's School of Public Affairs, brought together leaders in the fields of military and commercial technology. The purpose of the meeting was to gain insight into the risks and vulnerabilities inherent in the use of information technology on the battlefield and in military systems. This volume presents the results of that workshop.

During the last two decades of the 20th century, through a series of internal and external studies and policy pronouncements, the Department of Defense dramatically shifted its view of the nature of future military operations and the associated equipment, doctrine, tactics, and organization that were required. The names varied ("Reconnaissance/Strike Warfare," "Revolution in Military Affairs," "Network Centric Warfare," "Transformation"), but the basic premise was the same: The explosive changes in information technology would transform the future of military operations. The benefits of this change have been well documented, but its potential vulnerabilities have been less commonly described—or addressed for corrective actions. These actions must begin with a recognition of the new relationship between traditional defense systems and modern information technologies.

Traditional warfare systems are developed, ruggedized, hardened, secured, and tested to ensure the highest level of performance and availability. System development processes require configuration management and documentation processes that are maintained throughout the system life cycle. As military systems become more software intensive (in both computers and communications), greater time and cost increases occur because of increased system complexity and the lack of vigorous software processes, especially when compared with more mature, hardware-intensive engineering and development processes. For the most part, military systems are proprietary and communicate securely with little effect on performance. Current military weapons and combat platform system acquisitions have very high costs and extremely long lead times. This high expense and long preparation is attributed, in part, to the complexity of new system designs and to the rigidity of design processes that are needed to meet mission-critical battlefield requirements of high reliability, ease of maintenance, and built-in safety systems. The acquisition process itself introduces costs and delays because it must meet legal and regulatory demands designed to ensure openness and fiscal responsibility. These methods have produced formidable systems; American superiority in high-tech weapons development is acknowledged worldwide.

In contrast to military systems, commercial information systems can be developed, marketed, and upgraded within a 2-year life cycle. These systems are often not ruggedized, and some have failure rates higher than systems used by public safety or national security organizations. Decisions on system life cycle design are based on profit-and-loss statements for commercial enterprises where just-in-time component delivery, slightly degraded performance and system response rates, and increased repair times are considered acceptable. Frequently, factory tested or beta versions of new systems are fielded and tested in actual operational environments. Software flaws or operational glitches are either corrected with software patches or left in the field until new versions are developed. Commercial off-the-shelf (COTS) systems regularly are used without ownership of, knowledge of, or access to source and application code. That same code is often developed overseas, with minimal documentation, configuration management, or both. The introduction and adoption by industry of new technologies such as wireless, voice over Internet protocol (VOIP), and radio frequency identification devices (RFID) are rapid, with little design concern for security and privacy. Introduction of this technology in the commercial market is based on user acceptability, legal consequences, and bottom-line cost analysis, not on considerations of safety, potential loss of life, or national security policy.

In spite of these potential problems with commercial systems, their advantages—rapid deployment of state-of-the-art technology (consequently, higher performance) and far lower cost (because of much higher volume)—make them extremely attractive. Thus, over the past decade, Defense Acquisition Reform has been focused on developing processes to achieve both the high-performance and low-cost benefits that come from using commercial technology while still assuming the necessary mission objectives of high reliability, rugged environmental capability, and (particularly) security.

The challenge for the transformed military is to use information technologies to build a highly adaptive, high performance, and interoperable system infrastructure that is resilient, degrades slowly (if at all) under attack, and reconstitutes itself in a secure mode while under attack. To accomplish this challenge, this transformed military needs a better understanding of the life cycle vulnerabilities of information technologies. At the same time, as strategies for defense in the postmodern era are developed, consideration must be given to changing warfare system requirements to meet changing enemy threat scenarios so we understand how new threats affect system designs and vulnerabilities.

This volume examines threats and vulnerabilities in the following four areas:

- physical attacks on critical information nodes
- electromagnetic attacks against ground, airborne, or space-based information assets
- cyber attacks against information systems
- attacks and system failures made possible by the increased level of complexity inherent in the multiplicity of advanced systems.

Chapter 1, "Trends in Vulnerabilities, Threats, and Technologies," by Dr. Jacques S. Gansler and William Lucyshyn, provides an overview of the information technology issues on which the workshop focused. This chapter outlines the scope of information technology systems and services now being used in network centric military architectures. These architectures, if put into use as planned, will allow shared situation awareness, improve the quality and breadth of battlefield information, and provide commanders with the flexibility and mobility to find otherwise-survivable locations.

The authors trace the history and increased use of sophisticated information technologies in the battlefield and their relative success from Operation *Desert Storm* in 1991 to the present. They point out that, to meet the network centric warfare (NCW) goal of improving mission objectives by getting everyone "on the Net," organizational and doctrinal changes must be put into effect, processes reengineered, and education and training programs carried out, especially at the tactical levels. The authors also note that reliance on information technology and shared commercial networks in the battlefield raises concerns about attacks on the Nation's military forces and civilian infrastructures. They conclude that our ability to protect these new networks and communications links has not kept pace with our ability to develop them.

In chapter 2, "Physical Vulnerabilities of Critical Information Systems," Dr. Robert H. Anderson extends the scope of the workshop from military operations at the operational level of war to include homeland defense and critical infrastructure. He points out, and supports statistically, the economic and cultural effect of attacks against the infrastructure and, thus, includes its protection as a battlefield component. In addressing physical attacks, Dr. Anderson focuses on three design vulnerabilities:

- singularity, which addresses uniqueness and commonality of design
- separability, which prevents communication, reconstruction, and distribution of information
- accessibility, which addresses the ability to find and attack a physical entity.

The chapter explores the use of different mechanisms, such as biometrics, that can be used to limit access to either systems or facilities, but the discussion also points out the limitation of these technologies in a warfare environment. Dr. Anderson reminds readers that physical, kinetic effects (e.g., blast) are still the major means of attack and that bombs of all types can be created from easy-to-acquire materials. Physical, kinetic attacks, as we have learned from experience, can use low technology but still be highly effective. Dr. Anderson concludes his chapter with three recommendations for how to harden facilities and systems for military and homeland defense use:

- Design and build underground facilities or blast deflecting bunkers and other architecture.
- Ensure physical replication and redundancy (e.g., of network links and connectivity).
- Explore and support the development of grid computing, decentralized data storage, use of resilient Internet architecture, and peer-to-peer computing.

Chapter 3, "Physical Vulnerabilities Exposed at the National Training Center," by COL John D. Rosenberger, USA, was provided to the attendees as a precursor to the workshop. COL Rosenberger's chapter provides an example of the challenges and vulnerabilities of advanced technology warfare elements when they are used in the main defense in rugged terrain environment against a knowledgeable adversary. This document is referenced throughout the presentations and provides a resource for understanding not only some of the actual problems of technology integration in combat but also the importance of testing this technology in war games before executing major doctrine changes in warfare methodology.

Although COL Rosenberger supports and understands the power that NCW and its enabling information age technologies bring to the battlefield, he also identifies the limitations and inherent vulnerabilities of these systems. He warns that revolutionary changes, whether to systems or organizations, require careful analysis, testing, and exploration of all possible use scenarios to identify vulnerabilities. COL Rosenberger points out the need for a dual thrust for military transformation that continues to develop technologies but also maintains and improves development and training of our forces. He concludes his chapter with the following three recommendations:

- Pursue a strategy of blended complementary capabilities that includes a "robust" suite of unmanned airborne and ground sensors and combined-arms reconnaissance units that are embedded in every tactical command.
- Submit future designs, whether systems or organizations, to rigorous countermeasures during the testing phase to ensure that deployed systems are protected or can mitigate effects of attacks.
- Continue a training program that teaches our soldiers and marines how to perform basic military maneuvers such as map reading, navigation, and how to operate when IT systems are disrupted.

Chapter 4, "Dealing with Physical Vulnerabilities," by Bruce W. MacDonald, begins with a description of the blending of physical and cyber attacks to defeat or disrupt military information systems. He provides examples of how physical means can be used to insert cyber agents into information systems that lead to cyber attack and vice versa. Mr. MacDonald goes on to discuss nodal attacks capable of producing disproportionate effects in a military network centric architecture where the Global Information Grid (GIG) will reign as one of the most important major weapon systems in the U.S. arsenal. In this complex environment, Mr. MacDonald notes that the challenge to the battlefield commander is how to manage vulnerability and risk to attain mission success. He expresses concern that risk decisions are delegated to people who have vested interest in the outcome of the assessments and suggests that players with the appropriate scope of skills and resources are needed to assess system risks as part of the entire military enterprise.

The chapter reiterates the recurring theme of the workshop: As network centric designs expand, vulnerabilities must be mitigated to ensure that our ability to understand the battlefield is intact. A revolutionary approach to integrating current Information Technology systems into battlefield weaponry may make us more vulnerable and possibly unable to restore critical components if parts of our networks are attacked or compromised. Mr. MacDonald concludes with the following recommendations:

- Decentralized information systems must be capable of graceful degradation, resiliency, and self-healing.
- Metrics must be developed to improve risk assessments. Metrics should include improved modeling and field-testing.
- Security assessments and testing should be performed by independent, qualified personnel with the proper range of skills and resources.

Chapter 5, "Vulnerabilities to Electromagnetic Attack of Defense Information Systems," by Dr. John M. "Mike" Borky, addresses vulnerabilities the military faces as part of its commitment to IT as a key enabler of decisive, effects-based operations. Dr. Borky focuses on the vulnerability of friendly computer networks, telecommunications, and information systems such as the Global Positioning System (GPS) to disruption or damage from electromagnetic (EM) exposure. He points out that EM weapons are available, as was recently seen in the Iraq conflict, and that U.S. systems, especially those that rely on information technology, are potentially vulnerable to attack by these devices—including attacks by less sophisticated opponents. In asymmetric warfare, opponents will rely on low-cost electronic weaponry that can be used to disrupt, corrupt, and even physically damage military targets. The problem is magnified because of the large number of EM devices that are candidates for creating this type of weaponry and because of the even greater disparity in the EM susceptibility of different electronic systems.

To present his case, Dr. Borky postulates a simple model of command and control (C2) information processes using specific airpower centric scenarios emphasizing the operational, or theater, level of war. He then demonstrates how EM attacks can be effective in disrupting or damaging friendly C2 information systems that support these scenarios through jamming methods, deception, or delivery of electrical transients to sensitive electronics. From these examples Dr. Borky concludes that threat mitigation for the development of military IT systems must be based on careful design elements that include a range of design areas, from lightning protection to the development of robust software applications. Additionally, these systems should be subjected to controlled testing that includes exposure to simulated EM weapon transients and instruments to determine how the systems would respond to EM weapons attack.

In a worst case scenario, these weapons can lead to tactical success of the enemy, but in a lesser role, they can cause temporary disturbances in the C2 nodes that maintain operational pictures for commanders and exercise control of forces. In closing, Dr. Borky recommends the following:

- a layered defense in which each element of an integrated information system is designed for maximum hardness against EM effects without unduly compromising performance or cost
- continual monitoring of the status of and trends in EM weaponry by nations and organizations hostile to U.S. interests
- developing and deploying sensor and communications systems that can defeat hostile attempts to prevent the collection and distribution of this information.

Chapter 6, "Vulnerabilities to Electromagnetic Attack of the Civil Infrastructure," by Donald C. Latham, complements Dr. Borky's chapter by focusing on the vulnerabilities of the civil infrastructure that collects, manipulates, and delivers information products and services in support of both weapons and military operations. He points out the design vulnerability of many civil sector facilities such as communication centers, satellite ground control centers, and industrial control facilities to EM attacks. Mr. Latham laments the fact that Americans lack an understanding of U.S. military reliance on critical civilian infrastructure for the movement of troops, equipment, and supplies to overseas locations. He calls for better understanding of the effect of an EM attack on power supplies, ports or railroads, and other facilities, and then expounds on the ease with which this kind of attack can be accomplished. Using information readily available through the Internet and other sources, Mr. Latham walks the reader through several scenarios for attacks on critical infrastructure that could be carried out with little cost, low visibility, or both. Using the same publicly available tools and information, he shows how easily a hostile entity can recreate the physical topology of critical infrastructure such as financial and telecommunication systems.

Mr. Latham advises that a prioritized approach to civil infrastructure protection must be developed and suggests that the prime organization responsible for this activity be the Department of Homeland Security (DHS). DHS can succeed in developing a critical infrastructure vulnerability assessment and the policies on who pays for EM protection of facilities, but only with support from DOD and civil industries considered critical to U.S. national and economic security. Mr. Latham gives examples of tax-based from the telecommunications industry that are used to improve the survivability of certain DOD nuclear command, control, and communications lines and their associated facilities. To help mitigate EM attacks against the critical infrastructure, Mr. Latham recommends the following:

- multifaceted solution that addresses more thorough vetting of employees with critical access to telecommunications, networks, computers, servers, and other related equipment and software
- continued DOD analysis of vital civilian infrastructure that addresses mitigation strategies to avoid disruption in their capabilities and operations
- efforts to tackle difficult policy issues such as funding, ownership, and dual-use and dual-pay concepts by using existing financial models to address the challenges involved in who pays and how.

Chapter 7, "Trends in Cyber Vulnerabilities, Threats, and Countermeasures," by Michael A. Vatis, explores the threat to U.S. critical infrastructure posed by cyber attacks. Identifying the risk to military and public infrastructure, Mr. Vatis points out the lack of a nationwide strategic approach to defending against cyber attacks. To develop his position, Mr. Vatis illustrates a series of attacks launched against various industries and the military by threat agents that range from script kiddies to foreign nations. Mr. Vatis points out that several foreign nations have already developed information or cyber warfare doctrine, programs, and capabilities for use against one another, the United States, and other nations. He advises that the United States has and will continue to use offensive information warfare against its enemies for tactical purposes such as disabling command, control, and communications networks or disrupting anti-aircraft systems. Mr. Vatis suggests that, if policy with respect to broader uses of information warfare is finalized in National Security Presidential Directive 16, then the United States also may extend its defense against the use of cyber attacks to broader targets such as critical infrastructures. Therefore, Mr. Vatis concludes that the United States will continue to be the target of cyber attacks by adversaries seeking to strike our perceived Achilles heel—our dependence on information technology for the operation of critical government and civilian infrastructures and our military transformation.

Mr. Vatis notes that both the public and government need to recognize the effect that sophisticated cyber attack might have on military command, control, and communications systems during peacetime or military conflict and that a strategy needs to be developed to address cyber threats. Mr. Vatis concludes his chapter by emphasizing the need to understand potential mechanisms that Federal and State governments could use to improve the state of security. He suggests a range of solutions from direct regulation to development and use of general standards or best practices for hardware and software manufacturers of certain critical industries. After the decision is made about where responsibility and accountability for identifying and resolving cyber attacks should reside, Mr. Vatis proposes the following three activities:

- Develop the ability to detect an adversary's preparation for or launch of a cyber attack early enough to take steps to defeat it or to contain damage.
- Develop countermeasures to reduce risk and make the critical infrastructure less vulnerable to attack.
- Initiate research that includes analysis of corporate and government systems' risk and effect on enterprises to better understand the risks and economic costs that stem from cyber insecurity.

Chapter 8, "Enhancing Cyber Security for the Warfighter," by Sean R. Finnegan, addresses IT security vulnerabilities. Mr. Finnegan begins his chapter with a discussion of the need to put into effect current best practices used in information technology systems, such as installing firewalls and keeping them properly configured, as well as maintaining strong border protection. Mr. Finnegan points out, however, that some vulnerabilities will not be possible to fix and that other vulnerabilities have not yet been identified. He adds that legacy systems have limited security mechanisms and reduce the trust level of systems with which they interconnect.

Mr. Finnegan sets the stage for his chapter by describing the potential effect of a dedicated cyber attack from an adversary using an unknown exploit in a DOD system. If this cyber attack is a "stealth" attack in which the adversary makes every attempt to conceal the attack, the ramifications can be significant. The attack could continue until a sufficient mass of systems are compromised and critical DOD capabilities are disrupted. This type of "zero day" attack is feasible and, as Mr. Finnegan demonstrates, will make border defense and download of known patches ineffective because the attacker will have already breached the protected enclave. Mr. Finnegan suggests that it will take a combined DOD-vendor effort to produce a solution to restore systems that have been attacked in this manner to a secure state.

Mr. Finnegan shows how the increasing use of the Internet within national defense establishments allows attackers to analyze and exploit the interconnectivity of even closed networks and to launch distributed attacks from anywhere in the world. Access methodologies and protocols allow adversaries to mask their true identity by routing these attacks through unwitting hosts. He points out that processes such as the common criteria certification and the Microsoft FIPS 140 evaluations could be valuable if they were faster to use and were less costly.

Among the recommendations to improve system security are the following:

- Revive fundamental research to make programming less error prone and to create systems that are self-repairing and self-maintaining.
- Institute universal use of best practices such as Microsoft Secure Windows Initiative methodology, which is designed to improve software code security.
- Perform DOD analysis on ways to remove legacy products and reduce protocols and other security risks by adopting newer products such as IPSec and information systems management infrastructures.

Chapter 9, "Complexity of Network Centric Warfare," by Dr. Stanley B. Alterman, addresses the complexity of modern IT-based networks used in the design of a networked, information-age battlefield. This battlefield relies on information processing power to deliver the command, control, communications, computers, intelligence, surveillance, and reconnaissance (C4ISR) capabilities needed to establish decision superiority. Dr. Alterman suggests that the term "web centric" replace "net centric" as a more useful description of the current transformation effort, because value-added information that supports battlefield decisions will be available by access to networked nodes or URLs where real-time, dynamic information will be "posted." To attain this information-rich capability, the military must develop a system-level architecture that presents a single, time-sensitive, unified picture of the battlefield. Transformation, Dr. Alterman points out, is not the interconnectivity of stovepiped systems but, rather, a radical approach to building a ubiquitous and robust GIG that will allow decisions to be made at the operational level. This transformation will be accomplished with the aid of decisionmaking tools to prevent information overflow. The complexity of these systems and the difficulty in developing them can be offset by the use of different stages of product improvement or spiral development.

Dr. Alterman sets the stage for the complexity of the transformation effort by identifying seven new and reconfigured units and the many programs, initiatives, and demonstrations that are under way to support them. With each effort, Dr. Alterman identifies "complexity" hurdles that must be overcome for the transformation vision to become a reality. They include a range of organizational, operational, and technical issues. Dr. Alterman concludes his chapter with the following recommendations:

- Evolve joint doctrine so data ownership does not impede operations.
- Create a separate agency to manage the network centric systems effort.
- Allocate money to buy NCW systems jointly and ensure funding is available to support demonstrations and development of necessary technology.

Chapter 10, "Difficulties with Network Centric Warfare," by Dr. Charles Perrow, builds on the complexity issues discussed by Dr. Alterman. Dr. Perrow, an organizational theorist, discusses the complexity of NCW and warns of problems caused by emphasizing technology without looking at innovative approaches to strategy and tactics. He prefaces his discussion by defining problems associated with "interactive complexity" of systems. He focuses on two specific areas of NCW: stovepiping and micromanagement.

Dr. Perrow advises that a major part of innovation solutions is to problem solve through several autonomous sources rather than one centralized approach. This method allows a "best" solution to be identified from a range of solutions based on differing skill sets of the different agencies. Applying this model to NCW, Dr. Perrow reasons that systems are built to address needs and skills of various agencies and that logical interdependency of systems is impossible for just that reason. This weakness frequently causes rejection or misuse of new systems. When new systems are fielded, Dr. Perrow points out, they are more difficult to change and dismantle than individual stovepiped systems and can become a single target to adversaries. While Dr. Perrow understands the need for NCW, he also acknowledges that successful systems are initiated locally, they evolve, they are costly, and they are simple. He suggests that expectations for NCW should follow this model.

Delegation of authority, according to Dr. Perrow, is one of the best innovations of bureaucracies and information management. He points out that information—its ownership, volume, and credibility—is most useful when it is minimized and screened as it moves up the chain. Minimizing and screening information not only reduce workload but also prevent micromanagement by higher units. Companies that do not compress data are plagued with micromanagement and are at risk when management decisions are elevated above the level of expertise. Dr. Perrow's analysis indicates that NCW does not address the subject of information compression. He provides four examples of scale-free systems in which units can be interconnected without increasing hierarchy, and he discusses how information tiers used in these systems radically decentralize information and allow self-organization as well as autonomy at lower levels. He then addresses how these models could apply to NCW.

Dr. Perrow reminds readers that successful systems evolve through trial and error as well as cultures that allow change and allow leaders to support the grand strategies developed by senior executives. He closes with these recommended actions for DOD:

- Undertake a rigorous analysis of organizational, strategic, and tactical implications of NCW operations.
- Explore scale-free models for NCW application.
- Evaluate implications of "interactive complexity" in NCW efforts.

The conflicts in Afghanistan and Iraq demonstrate the power of information technology in warfare. Turning back is not an option. Network centric warfare is key to the military's future. However, the chapters in this volume also demonstrate the vulnerabilities and limitations of this technology. Renewed efforts are needed to find ways to protect these assets, to make them redundant if necessary, and to operate without them should they fail.

Chapter 1

Trends in Vulnerabilities, Threats, and Technologies

Jacques S. Gansler and William Lucyshyn

The Information Revolution

For much of the last decade, the world has been striving to adapt to the tidal-wave-like changes brought about by the dramatic improvements in information and communications technology, particularly as offered by the Internet. These changes have had a dramatic effect on the economics of information and have created new business models that have resulted in a new information economy. Companies are exchanging goods, services, and information in new ways that are more efficient and that are blurring geographic and geopolitical boundaries.

The Department of Defense (DOD) is embracing this information revolution. The hope is to leverage these new technologies and business models in ways that will transform the military to increase combat capabilities and to gain maximum advantage relative to potential adversaries. DOD currently operates 2 to 3 million computers, 100,000 local area networks, and 100 long distance networks that include systems used for the command and control of forces, systems to support distributed collaborative planning for crisis and contingencies, systems to manage logistics and supplies, and systems to distribute sensitive intelligence in real time.[1]

This approach has inherent risks. The technologies and resultant environment are evolving so rapidly that it is difficult, if not impossible, to fully digest, adapt, and incorporate changes before newer and better capabilities are developed. Incorporating these changes is especially difficult in the context of the military, where operational concepts and doctrine are prone to change very slowly.

Operation *Desert Storm*, however, provided a vision of things to come. The 6-month buildup provided enough time to innovate and incorporate some of the recent advances in digital technology to permit a degree of connectivity and integration not previously possible. Ad hoc architectures, based on commercial and prototype capabilities, were created and proved pivotal in the command and control of coalition forces and their subsequent victory. The extensive air campaign, for example, launched 2,240 sorties per day—more than 90,000 during the entire conflict. Eleven E–3A Airborne Warning and Control System (AWACS) aircraft controlled these sorties without a single midair collision. Using digital satellite data links, this entire air picture was made available, in real time, inside the Pentagon. An impressive constellation of more than 60 satellites—commercial, military, domestic, and international—was used to provide communications, intelligence, and navigation support. During *Desert Storm*, the precision navigation capabilities of the Global Positioning System (GPS) were used extensively for the first time,and this achievement enabled precision attacks on critical Iraqi targets and secured the movement of coalition forces across miles of featureless desert.[2]

These revolutionary warfighting concepts were further developed during the 16-month Afghanistan campaign and then again in the U.S.-led effort Operation *Iraqi Freedom*. Estimates indicate that the forces in Iraq for Operation *Iraqi Freedom* required 10 times the communication bandwidth used during Operation *Desert Storm*.[3] The increasing technological sophistication of U.S. forces also was evident during *Desert Storm*, when approximately 10 percent of the total number of weapons used were precision weapons. In Afghanistan, the percentage of precision weapons used increased to 60 percent of the total, and during *Iraqi Freedom*, the percentage was approximately 75 percent.[4] Many of these weapons were fitted with GPS-equipped Joint Direct Attack Munitions (JDAM) kits, allowing them to be used even when visibility was obscured.[5] The recent Iraq conflict also saw the first operational deployment of the 4th Infantry Division, the Army's most technologically sophisticated and digitized division.

In an effort to capture and articulate the goals for the future military transformation, the Chairman of the Joint Chiefs of Staff first published Joint Vision (JV) 2010, then a revised JV 2020.[6] These publications outline a vision for the transformation of the military that involves full incorporation of new technologies and capabilities and identifies information superiority as the key enabler to achieve the desired full-spectrum dominance.[7] JV 2020 recognizes that U.S. military forces must take advantage of superior information that is available, convert it to superior knowledge, and then achieve "decision superiority," which is defined as "better decisions arrived at and implemented faster than an opponent can react, or in a noncombatant situation, at a tempo that allows the force to shape the situation or react to situations and accomplish its mission." The emphasis on information superiority is clearly intertwined with the need to develop and ensure the ongoing development of new technologies.

Network Centric Warfare

Information superiority is, in itself, not a new objective. Centuries ago, Sun Tzu famously pronounced, "If you know the enemy and know yourself, you need not fear the result of a hundred battles." How is this concept modernized? Network centric warfare (NCW) is the military's attempt to harness the capabilities made available by the Information Revolution to provide commanders and combatants at every level an unprecedented view of the battlefield. However, NCW implies more than just incorporating the latest information technologies; it also addresses how missions are accomplished, how units are organized, how they relate to one another, and how they are efficiently and effectively supported. A large element of the concept involves effecting the transition from a platform centric orientation to a network centric orientation, where all the military forces are networked. The basic idea that sharing information is a source of value, while seemingly simple, has powerful implications.

Robert Metcalfe, founder of 3Com Corporation, observed that the new information technologies become more valuable as more people use them—an observation that has been postulated as Metcalfe's Law, which states that, although the cost of adding nodes to a network increases linearly, the utility of a network increases proportionately with the square of the number of users. Metcalfe's Law was demonstrated best by the explosive growth in the numbers of Internet sites and users and the associated utility. Within the context of military operations, Metcalfe's Law would imply that, as the number of military users added to the network increases, the value of the network would increase dramatically. Under these conditions, for example, military platforms on the network may not require their own organic sensors but may be able to take advantage of networked sensors.

The direct benefits of networking are difficult to quantify but have been demonstrated in military operations, exercises, and experiments. The first benefit is a shared situational awareness that leads to an ability to self-synchronize and results in an order of magnitude increase in the organization's performance. Forces that operate with shared battlespace awareness will have a significant operational advantage. The second benefit is a quantum improvement in the quality of the information that is rooted in the ability to fuse the information from all available battlefield sensors. This improvement will lead to the ability to make better decisions more rapidly, resulting in greater effectiveness with fewer friendly fire incidents. Units also will be able to operate more independently and still support an overall coordinated effort. Finally, commanders will have greater flexibility and mobility in choosing their command locations, thereby making the locations more survivable.

An evaluation of the Joint Tactical Information Distribution System (JTIDS) on 10,000-plus sorties revealed that when F–15s and AWACS aircraft shared a common air picture, the kill ratios increased by a factor of approximately 2.6—an increase in air-to-air combat power of over 100 percent. The JTIDS's data link allowed all of the fighters to share their radar information with one another and with the AWACS aircraft, so if one F–15 picked up an enemy aircraft, all the other friendly aircraft could see it.[8] Congressional reports further attest to the improvement: "A close analysis of the evidence has highlighted that new tactics, techniques, and procedures (e.g., new warfighting models)—enabled by dramatically improved capabilities for information sharing—play a key role in increasing combat power."[9]

Although the Services are still a long way from having fully implemented NCW, they have embraced that goal to achieve the vision of information superiority, and they appear committed to it. Fully developing the concept of network centric warfare means much more than simply inserting the latest information technology into battlefield-ready equipment, although technology will play a key role. Fully functional NCW requires a level of interoperability, not only at the strategic levels, which has already been achieved, but also at the tactical levels, which is not currently available. More important, NCW requires organizational and doctrinal changes as well as reengineering of processes, along with requisite education and training programs, to optimize how the mission can be better accomplished with everyone "on the Net."[10]

Digitally Networked Battlefield

The path to a network centric warfare capability has, at its foundation, a large-scale networking and digitization of combat systems that ultimately will create a digitally networked battlefield. The goal is for soldiers, airmen, sailors, marines, and their commanders to have a vastly superior situational awareness so they encounter far less "fog" on the battlefield than their predecessors. Under this concept, the battlefield will be monitored closely by a multisensor command and control constellation, which will include space-borne imaging and communications systems; manned and unmanned airborne platforms for reconnaissance and command and control; as well as ground-based surveillance and command, control, and communications systems. The sensor capabilities will range from satellite global imaging to advanced, man-portable, tactical battlefield radar systems that can detect vehicles and troops out to 100 meters.[11] All the vehicles operating on or above the battlefield, including fuel tankers, mess trucks, and bulldozers, will be equipped with advanced digital systems to improve their deployment efficiency.[12] Even individual soldiers will be equipped with a Land Warrior system, a digital system that will allow them to receive their orders, learn the disposition of friendly forces, and access intelligence—all displayed on GPS-integrated digital maps.[13] The objective is to provide the command elements a single integrated operations picture so virtually everyone on the network will be able to detect and identify friendly and enemy forces and their movements. With the capability to sense the battlefield in this way, commanders should be able to act first and seize the initiative, and units will be able to self-synchronize their actions.

New Vulnerabilities

These new capabilities do not come without a price (see chapter 3 for some lessons learned from the National Training Center). Our ability to protect these new networks and communications links, unfortunately, has not kept pace with our ability to develop them. As with any network system, some nodes will be more important than others; these critical nodes will have a high level of importance in the network and may have little or no redundancy. If attacked by an adversary, these nodes may create new vulnerabilities.

Several trends help to create these critical nodes. First, commercial information technology (IT) practices, which DOD tends to emulate, are to use the smallest number of servers possible. This criticality can be exacerbated by practices in the field where tactical units put their command and control elements in close proximity to one another in an effort to simplify physical connectivity. Second, budgetary constraints within DOD encourage standardization and uniformity rather than a more robust diversity of systems. When systems are uniform, then identifying a vulnerability in one allows an adversary to attack all similar systems. A third trend is the increasing dependence of the military on civilian telecommunications infrastructure. For example, during *Desert Storm*, over 90 percent of intertheater communications were supported using commercial satellites. The increased requirement for high bandwidth communications has magnified that requirement.[14] The need to use commercial satellites is a particular problem for platforms and mobile units that cannot physically connect to ground-based systems.[15] Yet with DOD's increasing reliance on civilian infrastructure, its vulnerability increases. If an adversary can identify and attack critical nodes, then it can degrade the networked capability and turn this new dependence into a potential weakness.

Another source of vulnerability is the increasing emphasis by DOD on the use of commercial off-the-shelf (COTS) systems and software. Many good reasons for using COTS products exist. Generally, when organizations use COTS systems and software, they minimize development risk, reduce "scope-creep," leverage the rapid commercial development cycle, and significantly reduce costs. However, as the use of COTS products expands, a vulnerability identified in a COTS system can be exploited to attack all the users of that same system. Additionally, the competitive nature of the IT business has driven many companies to outsource the development of code, with much of this work being done overseas. In all likelihood, engineers in overseas facilities could wind up developing COTS software that supports or is a major component in a sensitive U.S. military system. Checking these thousands and thousands of lines of code for all the functions they possibly may contain is difficult, so the possibility that this software has built-in Trojan horses or other viruses and trapdoors certainly does exist. As semiconductor and microprocessor production move overseas, the same issues exist. Hidden functions can be embedded; developers and operators tend not to test for things they do not know about.

The sheer volume of data that will flood these new networks introduces another potential vulnerability. The amount of data that is provided to a ground unit's tactical command post, for example, has grown exponentially from systems such as the global broadcast system, SHF Tri-Band Advanced Range-Extension Terminal (STAR-T), Secure Mobile Anti-Jam Reliable Tactical Terminal (SMART-T), and the AN/PSC–5 (UHF-VHF manpack line-of-sight satellite communications terminal).[16] If not properly managed and filtered, this information explosion can create more confusion than illumination. The extent of these networks, the large number of nodes, and the degree of access make them susceptible to

- exploitation by a creative, unsophisticated adversary

- intentional abuse by insiders
- any naturally occurring network failures
- physical capture.

Interdependencies between nodes also will occur, which are difficult to model and simulate and, consequently, will not be well understood or appreciated, introducing yet another source of vulnerability. Humans interacting with the systems can be an additional source of surprise events, either by introducing errors or by slowing down the processes by which errors are transmitted. Thus, humans can have a beneficial effect by functioning as dampeners and localizing effects.[17]

Another fallout of increasing technical sophistication is the growing disparity in our capabilities and those of our allies. As DOD continues to leverage developing information technologies, efforts to achieve coalition interoperability and to conduct coalition operations will become increasingly difficult.[18] When multinational operations are conducted, U.S. forces may have to regress to the level of the least capable, thus losing the advantage of their advanced capabilities. One final repercussion of the increasing levels of sophistication will be the introduction of both technical and organizational "complexity issues" along with the new capabilities technologies. A clever and determined adversary will learn to exploit these vulnerabilities.

Threats

Can a battlefield system connected to one network ever truly be safe? Information assurance threats to these systems can extend from conventional physical attacks at critical nodes to electromagnetic attacks against ground, airborne, and space assets and, finally, to cyber attacks against information systems. These attacks can be carried out by a broad spectrum of actors, ranging from teenage recreational hackers to nation-states or terrorist groups trying to gain strategic advantage. No matter how serious or well-trained the hacker is, the results can be the same—a disruption of military operations. The sophistication of the technology, coupled with the rate and volume of information transfer, will introduce a new level of vulnerability simply from the complexity of its combinations. In some cases, direct machine-to-machine interfaces may even cut humans "out of the loop." New potential exists for the unrecognized introduction of inadvertent and intentional (spoofing) errors that could interfere with mission accomplishment or possibly cause self-damage or friendly fire incidents.

Physical Threats

Although the line is blurring between the physical and cyber dimensions, the physical dimension is still very important. Physical attacks against key nodes—causing disproportionate effects—are an age-old military problem. Although many sophisticated techniques can be used to physically attack networks and communications systems, relatively primitive weapons can still be the most effective. Critical network nodes, satellite ground stations, and other dedicated military and commercial infrastructure can be attacked directly with high explosives or other physical means to disrupt military operations.

Additionally, transformed military operations of the type envisioned by DOD have extensive "reach back" requirements, which include logistics support. Attacks against U.S. forces, therefore, can be mounted in areas far removed from the theater of operations yet can still have a direct effect on combat operations. Because many of the details of support systems and operations are readily available on the World Wide Web, security achieved through obscurity is far more difficult. Moreover, many of the information and communication centers, as well as the people who man them, are difficult to duplicate; in many cases, critical integration details may have been developed locally and may not be well documented. Even if duplicated, a single backup can be insufficient if attacks come in clusters. These nodes would be attractive targets and, if successfully attacked, their vulnerability may have a disproportionate effect on U.S. military operations.

At the other end of the spectrum, if enemy forces capture one of the many individual computers that will be abundant in the future battlefield—possibly along with the legitimate user—adversaries may be able to access the battlefield networks and use that access to disrupt operations.

Electromagnetic Threats

The term electromagnetic threats covers a wide range of possible weapons that includes (a) "directed energy" such as electromagnetic pulse (EMP) and (b) electronic warfare. These weapons can destroy or incapacitate electronic systems without physical attack or explosives. The effects of one form of directed energy, EMP, were first observed during the last U.S. atmospheric nuclear test in 1962 (named "Starfish Prime"), which damaged electrical systems in Hawaii—800 miles away. This type of EMP, generated by nuclear weapons, can produce large electric fields over significant areas (depending on the altitude of weapon detonation) and has since been recognized as a threat to electronic systems.[19] Although measures can be taken to "harden" electronics to EMP, the susceptibility actually has increased because newer microchips using smaller feature sizes can be disrupted with smaller electric currents. Additionally, EMP can pose a significant threat to satellites. For example, a nuclear weapon detonated at high altitude could flood the Van Allen belt with electrons and disable all low, earth-orbiting satellites.[20]

Other forms of directed energy, even if not always acknowledged as such, are now a part of our everyday life. Advanced machine tools, laser pointers, fax machines, microwave ovens, and supermarket scanners all use a form of directed energy. If these same technologies are weaponized, they provide some unique capabilities to the user. Ground-based, high-energy lasers can be used to blind, or in some cases damage, satellite systems. High-power microwave weapons can be used for a wide range of effects, from upsetting electronics to destroying them in both military and commercial systems.[21] These weapons use high-power electromagnetic microwaves to penetrate military electronic systems through unintended pathways, causing either permanent damage or a temporary upset. A perverse hidden danger is that nondestructive effects can be used to achieve covert attacks, making it difficult or impossible to know whether a system has been attacked. Although weapons used to carry out these kinds of attacks are reasonably sophisticated, effective rudimentary weapons can be developed using commercially available sources. However, a lack of awareness of this problem is acknowledged in the commercial world and, therefore, commercial systems would be particularly susceptible. Although not currently a likely threat, laser or microwave weapons could be used effectively against command and control nodes to disrupt military operations or against commercial systems to cause economic strife.

Electronic warfare (EW), the oldest threat in the electromagnetic spectrum, is, in essence, warfare in the realm of communications. The history of EW goes back to the Battle of Britain and has been used in virtually every major conflict since. EW technologies and techniques can be used to deny the use of sensors and radio frequency communications.[22] Contrary to the impressions of many, advanced military technologies such as strike weapons aided by GPSs (e.g., JDAM) have increased both the desirability and potential benefits of EW for potential adversaries. The U.S. government recently has alleged that Russian companies sold GPS jammers to Iraq.[23] The operation of these jammers did not appear to hamper U.S. air operations during Operation *Iraqi Freedom*; apparently, they emitted enough of a signal to enable our forces to identify, locate, and target them, and one was even claimed to have been destroyed with a GPS weapon.[24] The quest for more effective jammers, however, is sure to continue.

Cyber Threats

Cyber attacks are an attractive alternative to other means used to defeat information systems. They offer the attacker the potential to play on a near-level playing field, and the effects can be disproportionate to the effort involved. The investment in resources is minimal, and, in most cases, the risk to the attacker is nonexistent. The attacker can be a hacker, an insider, a terrorist, a hostile nation-state, or a combination of these. When considering military operations, the motive for cyber attacks can range from creating mischief to "hacktivism" (hacking into sites to make a political statement) to espionage to the disruption of operations. Because all attackers use the same or similar techniques, identification of the motives is usually very difficult. Additionally, as the number of people with computer skills has increased and the hacking tools and techniques have become readily available to anyone with access to the Internet, the degree of technical sophistication required to successfully hack into a system has been reduced. As vulnerabilities are discovered in new products, they are first exploited and then shared with other attackers.

Cyber attacks can be launched from remote locations, offering the attackers a degree of anonymity and safety—much morethan for other direct attack methods. Advanced hackers can cover their tracks and make it difficult to identify not only who they are but also from where they are operating. They can use geographic, political, and administrative boundaries to great advantage. Law enforcement methods for investigating intrusion attempts are cumbersome as well as time consuming and would prove unsatisfactory in time of war—especially if battlefield systems were attacked.

As a result of these factors and in spite of the increased awareness and security measures, the number of attempted penetrations to Internet sites is steadily increasing. The number of hacking incidents reported worldwide has steadily increased from approximately 21,756 in 2000 to 52,658 in 2001 and 82,094 in 2002.[25] Because this reporting is voluntary, we can only assume that these figures are conservative and that they reflect only the trends in the numbers. A recent attack by the "ILOVEYOU" e-mail virus (technically also a worm) and its many variants penetrated 14 Federal agencies—including DOD, the Department of Energy (DOE), and the Central Intelligence Agency (CIA)—forcing many agencies to shut down their e-mail systems. The virus spread rapidly through DOD, infecting even classified systems and requiring many computers to have complete software reloads.[26] Several other well-publicized attacks against DOD systems have occurred, with varying degrees of success, but in every case it was difficult to identify and locate the sources of the attacks.[27]

Complexity of Threats

Digitizing the battlefield will have contradictory effects. On the one hand, it will improve situational awareness, significantly increasing the effectiveness of military forces. On the other hand, the quantity and sophistication of the technology introduced will increase significantly the level of complexity. From a technical perspective, as the complexity increases, the networks become less reliable and less predictable. Systems that are sufficiently complex can allow unexpected interactions of failures that defeat in-place safety systems. If these systems are tightly coupled, they can permit failures to cascade, sometimes enough to bring down the whole system.[28] This chain of events can be initiated by hardware failure, natural hazards, or, in the case of military operations, a deliberate attack on the system. More important, even when network systems work as designed, certain social and organizational issues will make it difficult to anticipate problems and control them.

One of the objectives of digitizing the battlefield is to create the potential for self-synchronization and independent contiguous operations. These depend on clear articulation of the commander's intent (the size of modern armies and their geographic dispersion necessitates this delegation to subordinate commanders). Yet the fast and real-time connectivity now possible could impose real-time micromanagement. The technology may impede traditional delegation rather than allow self-synchronization based on the delegated commander's intent.[29] This micromanagement of the battlefield, although technically possible, would not necessarily be desirable because it could focus senior leaders' attention on tactical details rather than on the operational and strategic picture. For example, it has been reported that, in the war on terror in Afghanistan, real-time targeting information was reviewed at Central Command Headquarters in Tampa, Florida. In several cases, suspected terrorists were able to escape when approval for the strikes was not received in time.[30]

The speed and complexity of the networked battlefield will make it necessary in some cases to take humans out of the decision loop. Air defense systems are one example. When these systems are configured to intercept surface-to-surface missiles—in which the window for a successful engagement is small—the rules of engagement can be programmed, and the interceptors will launch automatically. According to preliminary reports, the Patriot Advanced Capability–3 (PAC–3) systems deployed to Iraq have intercepted many Iraqi missiles launched at Kuwait. Yet they also shot down a British Tornado GR–4. Although the results of the investigation are not yet available, certainly one possible cause is an inadvertent automatic launch of the interceptor that occurred in response to faulty programmed rules.[31] Compressing the sensor-to-shooter cycle will create similar issues for other systems. This rapid decision cycle also can create the potential for spoofing and deception; an adversary with access to the friendly network could inject data to mislead forces.

Recommendations

The information revolution has had, and will continue to have, a dramatic effect on how military operations are conducted. As automated systems are fielded and the capabilities of the digital battlefield evolve, commanders will have the potential to make better decisions faster, which, ultimately, will increase their effectiveness. However, as NCW and the ubiquitous computing and networks that support it become fixtures on the battlefield, our adversaries will adapt and look for ways to exploit the new vulnerabilities created. As we come to depend on these capabilities, we must ensure that the integrity, confidentiality, and availability of the information on these networks and systems becomes as high a priority as deploying the systems themselves. The workshop arrived at the following recommendations: protect critical infrastructure, develop a system architecture, increase "red teaming," secure wireless technologies, develop security metrics, create the right incentives, monitor the threat, use an evolutionary approach, and improve security training. These recommendations are described in more detail in the following sections.

Protect Critical Infrastructure

The world is currently undergoing a transition to a new, borderless geography in cyberspace. As society grows more dependent on the Internet, that system's inherent vulnerabilities have put all of us—government, military, industry, and citizens—at risk. In this environment, it would not be wise to consider military operations in isolation from civilian information assurance issues. Private sector infrastructure, in many cases, directly supports military operations (with communications, logistics, etc.), and these must also be considered. These private sector systems, with all their benefits and problems, are increasingly being incorporated into military systems.

Develop a System Architecture

A systemwide network architecture is required because the various systems, coupled with the large number of organizations and stakeholders, make it difficult at times to maintain a view of the "big picture" while working on the parts. In the past, lack of an overall architecture has led to solutions being developed that are limited in scope, suboptimized, and not interoperable within and across organizations and services. The goal should be to create battlefield networks that are highly automated, adaptive, interoperable, and resilient to all types of attacks. These networks should achieve the following objectives:

- Design for graceful degradation. Battlefield systems should be developed with a degree of fault tolerance along with the capability to degrade gracefully. A concerted effort should be made to minimize the creation of critical nodes and move toward distributed systems. Likewise, a certain level of redundancy should be built into these networks.
- Design for robustness. An obvious first step in reducing cyber vulnerabilities within a system is to improve overall software quality. Identifying and preventing those products with easily exploitable vulnerabilities from being widely used will certainly reduce the more pedestrian attacks. Research should continue to develop automated tools to detect and mitigate malicious codes that may be embedded in COTS systems or that might be left behind in undetected attacks and, of course, to discover the capability to identify and nullify these codes.
- Ensure rapid reconstitution. Physical attacks can and often do target multiple sites; therefore, one backup site may be insufficient. Although diversity has benefits, recovery will be easier and faster with homogeneous, readily available systems. These two attributes must be balanced carefully. Another critical element—often neglected—that affects the ability to reconstitute systems is the people with unique knowledge or experience, especially with respect to integration issues. Rigid, documented configuration control will facilitate the refreshing of software systems in the event that less-experienced personnel must do the work.
- Design for security up front. Many security vulnerabilities in both hardware and software result from inadequate consideration of security during the design process. Information technology companies must be encouraged to carry out security training for de-

signers and software developers and improve their efforts to build in security up front.

Increase "Red Teaming"

One of the most effective ways for both the military and the private sector to ensure secure systems is to conduct frequent "red team" attacks on their own systems. These skilled, friendly attackers can identify vulnerabilities of systems, which then can be fixed before they can be exploited. Although a reluctance to test and identify weaknesses in one's own systems is natural, in the past, these efforts have proved extremely useful.

Secure Wireless Technologies

Laptops and other portable-wireless technologies need to be introduced to the battlefield slowly because they can introduce significant vulnerabilities. These vulnerabilities should all be tested independently and verified as having suitable safeguards. Although biometric authentication is good, it may be insufficient for battlefield use, and consideration should be given to including duress code (e.g., two different passwords). Then, if the equipment and operator are captured, the system can be identified as having been compromised. In addition, if they are captured, these systems can be populated with false data to obfuscate the true information.

Develop Security Metrics

DOD must monitor the effectiveness of its information assurance efforts by continuously benchmarking and tracking their progress with appropriate metrics. A simple, consistent metric that is easy to use and understand should be used to enable accountable supervision. These measures can be adapted and passed down through the organization and made directly relevant at all levels. Risk metrics should also be developed so units will know not only what threats are possible but also what threats are probable.

Create the Right Incentives

As DOD and the Federal Government attempt to influence the security practices of IT companies and other private enterprises, a key point that must be remembered is that things are the way they are for a reason. That is, proper economic incentives do not exist to develop secure software and systems or to maintain high levels of security. Only recently have commercial firms begun to pressure their software suppliers to provide far greater security. Much more attention needs to be paid to this area by commercial buyers in the future. The government has many tools in its kit bag, for example, the "bully pulpit," regulations, tax policy, grants and subsidies, etc., that can be used to create incentives for companies to voluntarily improve security practices, and these tools need to be explored and put to good use. For DOD, an emphasis on security for weapon systems can be added by identifying information assurance requirements within the acquisition process, namely, within DOD Directive 5000.1, "The Defense Acquisition System."

Monitor the Threat

One of the most effective ways to improve information assurance is to improve the intelligence on potential adversaries. Anticipating an attack will allow U.S. forces to preempt vulnerabilities. To effectively respond to threats that require specific equipment such as the dual-use hardware to improvise a high-power microwave weapon, that equipment should be added to the appropriate watch lists and its process should be tracked.

Use an Evolutionary Approach

To ensure that the military receives the full benefits from information technologies and the concept of network centric warfare, changes should be introduced in an evolutionary manner (i.e., so-called "spiral" development and deployment). This approach will allow the military doctrine and culture to change along with the technology without unintended consequences such as excessive micromanagement or increased vulnerability.

Improve Security Training

One of the most critical elements of any comprehensive information assurance program is the people who use and operate the systems. Whatever else is done, a continuing program must be put in place to promote the understanding of not only best practices, policies, and controls related to the issue of security but also the risks that prompted the adoption of those standards. Better understanding of the risks will allow senior personnel to make more informed decisions with respect to the resources required to protect their systems. The first line of defense, the users, must also understand the importance of complying with policies and controls.

Conclusion

Over the last 15 years, many claims have been made about a revolution in military affairs. Most have proved premature. Moreover, the claims have had no shortage of critics because military leaders have proved reluctant in the past to embrace unproven innovations. The information revolution, however, has truly touched and changed every aspect of our lives, including the military, in significant ways. We have grown to depend on our computers and networks and the advantages they provide. Although this path is not without risks, the U.S. military can and will adapt. This book is a plea for greater attention to the vulnerabilities of these systems and for a focus on countering these vulnerabilities. The security of our Nation depends on it.

Notes

[1] Robert F. Dacey, *Progress and Challenges to an Effective Defense-Wide Information Assurance Program*, GAO-01-307. (Washington, D.C.: General Accounting Office, March 2001).

[2] Barry R. Schneider and Lawrence E. Grinter, *Battlefield of the Future: 21st Century Warfare Issues*. (Maxwell Air Force Base, Alabama: Air University Press, 1998), 184–85.

[3] Vago Muradian, et al., "War Puts Transformation to Test," *Defense News*, March 24, 2003. Accessed at <www.defensenews.com>.

[4] Robert S. Dudney, "The U.S. Air Force at War," *Air Force Magazine*, May 2003, p. 2.

[5] Peter Pae, "War With Iraq/Military Technology," *The Los Angeles Times*, March 22, 2003, 14.

[6] Office of the Chairman, Joint Chiefs of Staff, *Joint Vision 2010* (Department of Defense: Washington, D.C., 1996) and *Joint Vision 2020* (Department of Defense: Washington, D.C., 2000).

[7] Information superiority is defined as the capability to collect, process, and disseminate an uninterrupted flow of information while exploiting or denying an adversary's ability to do the same.

[8] William B. Scott and David Hughes, "Nascent Net-Centric War Gains Pentagon Toehold," *Aviation Week & Space Technology*, January 27, 2003, 50–54.

[9] Arthur L. Money, "Report on Network Centric Warfare: Sense of the Report," submitted to Congress, March 2001.

[10] Ibid.

[11] Henry Kenyon, "Tactical RADAR Puts Teeth to Perimeter Security Mission," *Signal*, March 2000.

[12] Robert K. Ackerman, "Army Transformation Changes Force Targets for Digitization," *Signal*, July 2000.

[13] The Army had such confidence in these systems, that the 4th Infantry Division's vehicles deployed to Iraq in March 2003 with Force XXI Command Brigade and Below system before the initial operational test and evaluation could be accomplished. See Frank Tiboni, "U.S., U.K. Troops carry Force Trackers," *Defense News*, March 24, 2003, Accessed at <http://www.defensenews.com.>.

[14] The Pentagon estimates that current operations in Iraq will need 10 times the bandwidth used in Operation *Desert Storm*. See Vago Muradiam, et al., "War Puts Transformation to Test," *Defense News*, March 24th, 2003. Accessed at <http://www.defensenews.com.>.

[15] E. C. Helme III, *Diminishing the Critical Vulnerability of Space* (Newport, RI: Naval War College, February 1998).

[16] The global broadcast system is a space-based, high data rate communications link for the asymmetric flow of information from the United States or rear echelon locations to deployed forces. The SHF Tri-Band Advanced Range-Extension Terminal (STAR-T) provides the Army

with an HMMWVmounted, C–130 Roll-on–Roll-off, SHF multichannel Tactical Satellite Terminal (TACSAT). The terminal operates over both commercial and military SHF satellites and has joint Service applicability. The SMART-T system provides tactical users with secure, survivable, anti-jam, low probability of intercept and detection satellite communications in an HMMWV configuration. The program supports advancing forces as they move beyond the line-of-sight capability of Mobile Subscriber Equipment (MSE) and can use Milstar and commercial satellite communications links. The AN/PSC–5 is a UHF-VHF manpack line-of-sight and Satellite Communications (SATCOM) Demand Assigned Multiple Access (DAMA) Communications Terminal. This supports the DOD requirement for a lightweight, secure, network-capable, multiband, multimission, anti-jam, voice-imagery-data communications capability in a single package.

[17] Chris C. Demchak and Patrick D. Allen, "Technology and Complexity: The Modern Military's Capacity for Change," in *Transforming Defense*, edited by Conrad C. Crane (Carlisle, PA: Strategic Studies Institute, December 2001.

[18] John J. White, *Retrospect of Information Technology's Impact on Society and Warfare: Revolution or Dangerous Hype* (Newport, RI: Naval War College, February 4, 2003).

[19] Kenneth R. Timmerman, "U.S. Threatened with EMP Attack," *Investigative Report*, May 28, 2001, 16.

[20] The Van Allen belt is a region of high-energy particles, mainly protons, held captive by the magnetic influence of the Earth within 4,000 miles or so of the Earth's surface. It is a by-product of cosmic radiation. Joseph Anselmo, "U.S. Seen More Vulnerable to Electromagnetic Attack," *Aviation Week & Space Technology*, July 28, 1997, 67.

[21] Eileen Walling, *High Power Microwaves: Strategic and Operational Implications for Warfare* (Maxwell Air Force Base, Alabama: Center for Strategy and Technology, Air War College, February 2000).

[22] Martin Libicki, *What Is Information Warfare* (Washington, D.C.: Center for Advanced Concepts and Technology, 1995), 28–33.

[23] Kevin O'Flynn, "War in the Gulf: Russians Deny Baghdad Missile Sales," *Guardian Home Pages*, March 25, 2003, 6.

[24] "U.S. Weapons Easily Target Jamming Devices," *The Ottawa Citizen*, March 27, 2003, F5.

[25] Statistics are from the CERT Coordination Center. An incident may involve one site or hundreds (or even thousands) of sites. Also, some incidents may involve ongoing activity for long periods of time.

[26] Keith A. Rhoades, "'ILOVEYOU' Computer Virus Emphasizes Critical Need for Agency and Government-wide Improvements," GAO/T-AIMD-00-171, May 10, 2000.

[27] Jacques A. Gansler, "Protecting Cyberspace," in *Transforming America's Military*, edited by Hans Binnendijk (Washington, D.C.: National Defense University Press, 2002).

[28] Charles Perrow, "Organizing to Reduce the Vulnerability of Complexity," *Journal of Contingencies and Crisis Management 7 (3)* (September 1999).

[29] John White, *Retrospect of Information Technology's Impact on Society and Warfare: Revolution or Dangerous Hype* (Newport, RI: Naval War College, February 4, 2003.

[30] Julian Borger, "War in Afghanistan: U.S. Held Back From Attacks on Taliban," *The Guardian*, November 19, 2001, 3.

[31] Mike Toner, "War in the Gulf: Battle Tactics: Patriot Missile System," *The Atlanta Journal and Constitution*, March 26, 2003, A15.

Chapter 2

Physical Vulnerabilities of Critical Information Systems

Robert H. Anderson

A "digitized battlefield" and "military operations at the operational level of war" are key concepts of the ongoing Department of Defense (DOD) transformation and, as such, are important contexts for a discussion of current physical threats, vulnerabilities, and countermeasures. However, concentrating on such a narrow scope may skew the discussion. We have been told repeatedly that we are now at war—a war on terrorism. The "battlefield" is worldwide, with emphasis on the U.S. homeland. To ignore this battlefield while concentrating on military operations exclusively would be to miss the real threat: the physical, kinetic attack of September 11, 2001, caused more damage—economic, physical, and human—to the United States than could have been inflicted on a military battlefield. The economic damage from this one physical attack is now estimated at easily more than $100 billion and counting, with major institutions (e.g., United Airlines) in bankruptcy as, at least, a partial result of the attack.[1] Our airports, borders, and citizens have taken on a bunker mentality. Yet, even with all of the additional precautions, the level of vulnerability seems to have increased. We are, in fact, at war.

This chapter attempts to probe the minds of would-be attackers by asking, Where can a successful physical attack be executed within the United States to cause the most damage with the greatest effects? The conclusion is that hitting the country's "soft underbelly"—its economy, now teetering between recession and recovery, and the psychology of its citizens—would yield by far the greatest payoff. Therefore, any consideration of the modern battlefield must include critical homeland information infrastructures, especially those involved with the national financial and economic health.

The Threat = Actor + Motivation + Means

On the wider, modern battlefield, the actors range from individuals acting essentially alone (e.g., Timothy McVeigh in Oklahoma City) to loose confederations of "cells" of individuals working together (e.g., al Qaeda operatives executing the September 11 coordinated attacks). On a more narrowly conscribed military battlefield, the actors are our opponents—members of the opposition military as well as disgruntled and disaffected people within the local citizenry. The key difference is the fluidity of the new actors. They are enemies without borders who often lack discernible connections to any nation-state. Under conditions such as these, the battlefield is truly transformed.

The motivation for attacks on the larger-scale battlefield differs from the political and territorial objectives of historical wars. The individual motivations reflect the nature of the new actors.

Modern actors may attack targets solely for symbolic reasons, for publicity, or to make the United States look weak and vulnerable. An attack that has a substantial negative effect on the U.S. economy can fulfill all of these motivations, and such an attack should be considered a credible threat.

The means for physical, kinetic attack can be simple and relatively inexpensive. For the purposes here, this chapter considers the means of carrying out a physical, kinetic attack against critical infrastructures (especially those housing information system components) to be truck bombs of the type used in Oklahoma City or airplanes filled with fuel of the type used on September 11—with special attention on small, private aircraft that can target individual buildings. These smaller aircraft allow ready access to otherwise potentially inaccessible sites, for example, those surrounded by fences, barbed wire, barriers, or guards. And they are easier to learn to fly and procure for use than commercial airliners.

A second means of physical attack more relevant to the military battlefield is the capture and destruction or the use of critical "nodes" in a C4ISR military information system.[2] Obtaining a laptop or other client machine or server from the battlefield is one such example of a relatively simple strike. Although this possibility is addressed below, it appears to be less compelling as a threat because battlefield information systems have redundancy and various fail-safe measures built in. In addition, U.S. military personnel are trained to act autonomously and creatively in the absence of information and are regularly briefed on the possibility of terrorist strikes.

To date, physical attacks have been the most prevalent means for terrorists. Figure 2-1 shows the relative frequency of various modes of attack during a recent 1-year period.

Figure 2–1. **Frequency in the Use of Attack Weapons in Terrorist Attacks Source**

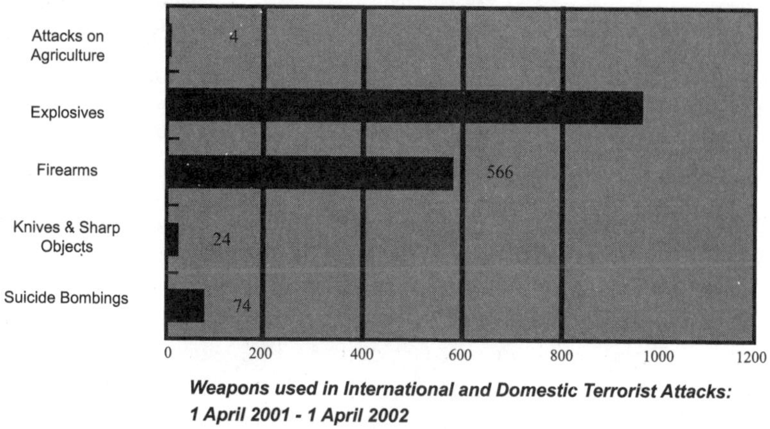

Source: Unpublished briefing by Kevin O'Brien, Rand Europe, derived from RAND Terrorism Chronology, accessible, in part, at http://db.mipt.org

Although other modes of attack such as biological and cyber may become increasingly widespread, "blowing things up" will likely remain a dominant form of attack, one for which "battle damage assessment" is easy, publicity (through highly photographable effects) is widespread, and effects are long lasting.

Vulnerabilities to Physical, Kinetic Attack

What attributes of a system make it vulnerable to a physical, kinetic attack? RAND research on the vulnerability of command and control as well as on the vulnerability of other complex information systems to a variety of attacks uses, as a starting point, the list of 19 generic attributes of a potentially vulnerable system that are shown in figure 2-2.[3] Other approaches to vulnerability assessment of critical infrastructures, separate from but similar to the methodology, are discussed in a series of documents published by the U.S. Department of Energy.[4]

Figure 2–2. **Attributes of a System Leading to Potential Vulnerability**

Design / Architecture:

- Singularity
    - Uniqueness
    - Centrality
    - Homogeneity
- Separability
- Logic / implementation errors; fallibility
- Design sensitivity, fragility, limits, finiteness
- Unrecoverability

Behavioral:

- Behavioral sensitivity / fragility
- Malevolence
- Rigidity
- Malleability
- Gullibility, deceivability, naiveté
- Complacency
- Corruptibility
- Controllability

General:

- Accessible, detectable, identifiable, transparent, interceptable
- Hard to manage or control
- Self-unawareness and unpredictability
- Predictability

In our vulnerability assessments, we typically search for these system attributes at various architectural levels within a system and in four domains:

- physical
- cyber
- human or social
- enabling infrastructure.

Of particular importance with respect to a physical, kinetic attack are the following attributes:

- singularity (including uniqueness, centrality, homogeneity)
- separability
- accessibility, detectability, identifiability, transparency, interceptability.

By singularity we mean equipment, facilities, or processes that have one or more of these attributes:

- Uniqueness—Singularity in availability; an object is the only one of its kind and, thus, not only is hard to replace but also may be less likely to have been thoroughly tested and perfected.
- Centrality—Singularity in location. Failure points are collected in a single place.
- Homogeneity—Singularity in type. Replication of multiple, identical objects share any common flaws or weaknesses.

The attribute of separability applies most directly to networks in which cutting one or perhaps two links can bifurcate the network into two portions no longer capable of communicating with each other. Accessibility is especially important for physical, kinetic attacks because these attacks require locality for their effects. But attacks from the air (either by dropping a bomb or by conducting a suicidal crash) on stationary facilities can provide a type of physical accessibility unhindered by traditional barriers, guards, gates, and fences.

The attribute of singularity takes on increased importance when considering physical, kinetic attacks because, if some facilities required by the system are unique, centrally located, or both and are damaged or destroyed in the attack, then replacement could take days, weeks, or even months—depending on the uniqueness of the equipment or facilities. One saving grace of modern information systems (at least for systems not specialized for the battlefield) may be the fact that they tend to be built from standard components: client personal computers (PCs), ethernet cables, T1 or T3 lines, servers, routers, and the like. Although there may be centrality in a facility, there is little uniqueness: The equipment can be replaced by commercial off-the-shelf (COTS) equivalents quickly, and the relevant software and databases are presumably backed up on physical media at a site sufficiently far removed that the same physical attack would not damage those backup media. Military battlefield information system equipment is also increasingly built from COTS equipment that can be replaced rather quickly or for which spares are deliberately stored and available.

The primary source of vulnerability to physical attack therefore would appear to be unique equipment or facilities that are physically accessible (e.g., by ground or air) and for which repairs or replacements of damaged elements would take an extended period of time.

Example: Critical Infrastructure

In the analysis of larger battlefield threats, the importance of symbolic targets that could also create major disruption to our economy was introduced. Clearly, vital information systems on which the U.S. economy depends tend to have mirrored backup sites to preclude a single point of failure. The New York and NASDAQ stock exchanges (highly symbolic of our economy) have backup facilities away from Manhattan that can take over in the event of a major physical attack on the primary facilities. Major banks such as Citibank have secondary (and tertiary, etc.) processing sites for key operations. In fact, in the aftermath of the World Trade Center attack, backup processing sites generally performed well, allowing quite rapid reconstitution of critical financial and market operations.

These systems' backup facilities would seem to mitigate or eliminate the key vulnerability of having a singularity (uniqueness or centrality) that could be attacked to great effect. However, what is often underappreciated is the demonstrated ability of terrorists to conduct dual, simultaneous attacks. The combined World Trade Center and Pentagon attacks of September 11 are only the most visible examples. But consider other simultaneous, coordinated attack events extending over the past 20-plus years:[5]

- 2003 attacks on separate expatriate housing complexes in Riyadh, Saudi Arabia
- 1998 simultaneous attacks on the U.S. embassies in Dar es Salaam, Tanzania, and Nairobi, Kenya
- 1993 series of bombings in Bombay
- 1983 attack on U.S. Marine barracks and French paratroop headquarters in Lebanon
- 1981 hijacking of three Venezuelan passenger jets
- 1970 Dawson's Field hijacking by the Popular Front for the Liberation of Palestine.

Judging by the ability of terrorist networks to conduct simultaneous attacks, clearly less safety and security exists in two mirrored (or otherwise backed-up) physical processing facilities than is often assumed.

As a concrete example, let us put ourselves into the role of a major terrorist group that is capable of conducting two or more simultaneous physical attacks of substantial magnitude—of size and scope similar to the 1998 embassy bombings. The intent would be to inflict substantial damage on trust in major economic institutions and the U.S. economy; to have a major symbolic effect with worldwide consequences; and to create damage for which recovery would be time-consuming and expensive, with major financial-economic effects during the duration. Many possible targets meet these criteria, for example, dual attacks on the NASDAQ or New York Stock Exchange processing centers, dual attacks on key facilities of any one of the top 10 national banking institutions, and multiple attacks on the secure networks that banks use to transfer funds among themselves. As a test case, the author used publicly accessible Web site information from an important financial institution. Using recruiting information available on the organization's Web site, he found several organization sites listed, some of which were candidates for key multiple processing centers for the organization. Using those sites as further search terms, he found articles on a Russian Web site (in Russian) and a European Web site providing further confirmation of the location of those processing centers and even giving the range of Internet protocol (IP) addresses assigned by the local Internet service provider (ISP) for one of the sites.

The locations of these multiple processing centers are nowhere mentioned in that organization's annual report or other printed documentation. Nevertheless, it is clear that attempts at security through obscurity are inevitably a losing proposition in this era of the Internet. Too many clues and cues are scattered loosely around the Web and can be pieced together in a few hours of Web surfing. (And, as a colleague pointed out, once one gets geographically near a surmised location, talks with a few area taxi drivers usually can resolve any ambiguity about location and address.)

Continuing the hypothetical test case, by gaining access to an organization's address, one can then find handy maps to the desired financial processing location from mapquest.com and other online atlases. Any terrorist with basic computer literacy and a desire to gain more information could respond to the company's recruiting ads and request information about the facilities, locations, equipment, processing, and so forth. A bit more reconnaissance would indicate that these sites are above-ground buildings providing reasonable access to a truck of the Oklahoma City variety or certainly to a small airplane on a suicide mission. It turns out that the described processing centers are in semirural areas, with considerable farming under way nearby. A panel truck with fertilizer and fuel oil might well go unnoticed until too late.

The point of this example is to indicate that systems absolutely critical to the economic well-being of the United States and other countries appear to be highly susceptible to simultaneous physical, kinetic attacks and to have transparent information about location and operation that, during a single session of Web surfing, allows one to make simple deductions with respect to operations.

Literally hundreds of other examples could be provided that indicate the vulnerability to physical attack within the U.S. or international critical information infrastructure. We conclude that, unless substantial steps are taken to mitigate these attacks, they will remain the simplest, most efficient means of attacking the United States as a symbol, as an economy, and as a means of gaining publicity (through the display of tangible, physical evidence) of the highest measure. Physical infrastructure attacks are credibly not only the most likely kind of attack to occur but also the attack with the highest potential degree of success.

Example: Military Battlefield

Military battlefields, of course, are full of enemies with weapons designed to inflict physical, kinetic damage. Mortars, rocket launchers, grenades, tank guns, and laser-guided bombs head a list of weapons that is practically endless. Yet battlefield command posts that contain valuable computer and information technology are often housed in shelters that cannot withstand a hit from any of these weapons. A notional next-generation battlefield information system is represented in figure 2-3.

Figure 2–3. **Military Battlefield Information System (Notional Schematic)**

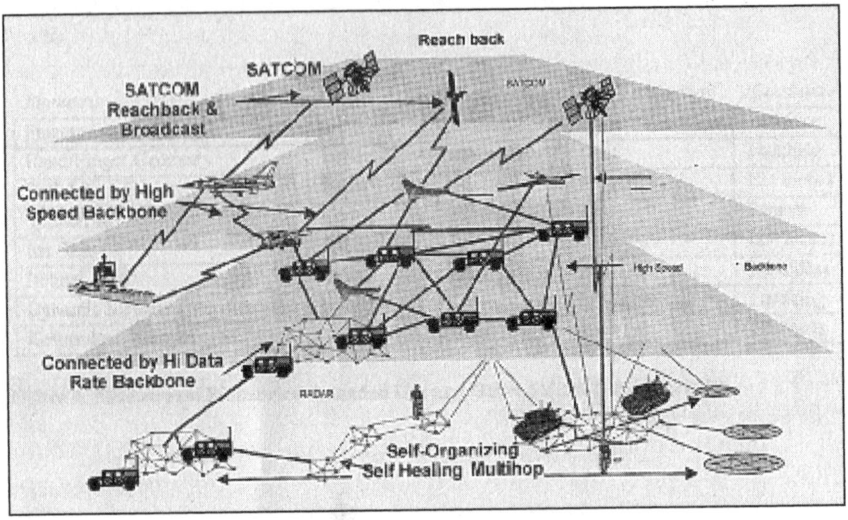

If attacked even by a relatively crude or simple weapon, any of the nodes or links in such a system could be physically damaged or destroyed. Most of the nodes have some form of redundancy that would permit rather rapid repair and reconstitution of the larger network and its information. The author has not performed sufficient analysis of system architecture such as that represented in figure 2-3 to assert whether single points of failure exist that would, if destroyed, critically affect the system's operation. But it appears likely that these networks will increasingly be self-organizing and self-healing to minimize damage.

Notwithstanding, another kind of physical damage can occur: the capture of physical equipment (e.g., client workstation, server, or other network node) that could lead to compromise of the system. The enemy might gain direct access to the system through the stolen device and, having access, would be free to implant false information, obtain information, and corrupt key databases or the processing itself. That threat is more insidious because it could be done in a manner that remains undetected.

One major thrust toward protecting against enemy access of military information system components is the use of biometrics—statistical testing of attributes of human physiology or behavior—to establish identity or verify it. Figure 2-4 shows examples of potentially relevant biometric products and their respective attributes as related to identity-verification abilities, robustness, distinctiveness (i.e., ability to identify or verify an individual uniquely), and intrusiveness.

Figure 2–4. **Mainstream Biometrics' Intended Use and Other Salient Characteristics**

Biometric	Identify vs. Verify	How Robust	How Distinctive	How Intrusive
Fingerprint	Either	Moderate	High	Touching
Hand/Finger Geometry	Verify	Moderate	Low	Touching
Facial Recognition	Either	Moderate	Moderate	12+ inches
Speaker Recognition	Verify	Moderate	Low	Remote
Iris Scan	Either	High	High	12+ inches
Retinal Scan	Either	High	High	1/n inches
Dynamic Signature Verification	Verify	Low	Moderate	Touching
Keystroke Dynamics	Verify	Low	Low	Touching

Because of the potential importance of biometrics in battlefield information system security and protection, DOD has established a Biometrics Management Office (BMO) whose function is to "consolidate, coordinate, and manage the effective test, evaluations, and incorporation of Biometrics in support of . . . combatant commanders, military services, and DOD agencies."[6] In one example case study involving 70 SIPRNet[7] and 70 NIPRNet[8] accounts and using the Identix BioLogon 2.03 system,[9] the BMO found a return on investment of 118 percent but concluded that command buy-in and support were essential to success and that a preinstallation training and awareness campaign was necessary to ensure broad support.[10] This study reflects findings from a specific implementation at a specific point in time. These findings may or may not be consistent with those of other biometric implementation.

However, a number of cautions warn about expecting biometric solutions to "solve" the problem of battlefield compromise of information system equipment. Among the cautions often cited are the following:

- Under battlefield conditions, dirt, sweat, contamination, worn equipment, and injuries could affect measurements such as fingerprint reading and keystroke dynamics.
- Even under reasonable conditions, the false-positive (identifying someone as authorized who is unauthorized) and false-negative (identifying someone as unauthorized who is authorized) instances are quite high for current biometric systems. Do we want these errors to occur under battlefield conditions where the decisions can mean life or death?[11]
- Often, one person must substitute quickly for another using a terminal or piece of equipment. (One colleague, in interviewing military personnel with respect to the potential effectiveness of biometric measures on the battlefield, often heard tales from previous wars "about cooks taking up guns to defend bases.") That may be a poor analogy for accessing a C4ISR system, but it is easy to imagine an emergency condition scenario where someone not formally authorized to use a system must substitute for someone who is logged in but becomes unavailable.

This author is currently unaware of any relatively foolproof and reliable method—that might not impair our own operations under battlefield conditions—of determining whether a node or link of a critical battlefield information system has fallen into enemy hands. The ongoing pursuit of these types of performance attributes likely will continue to be a challenge.

Remedies to Kinetic Attacks

Physical attacks, especially on critical infrastructure facilities of the kind represented by the financial organization example, are very hard to eliminate or remedy—especially when attack by suicide aircraft (even a small private plane) is a threat. Three types of remedy appear relevant and are discussed in turn:

- underground facilities or "blast deflecting" bunkers or architecture
- physical replication or redundancy (e.g., of network links and connectivity)
- grid computing, decentralized data storage, use of the Internet's resilient architecture, peer-to-peer computing.

Underground Facilities or Deflecting Bunkers

Most buildings housing critical information infrastructure facilities are normal, above-ground office-style buildings. Despite their fences and guards and gates, they are highly susceptible to physical, kinetic attacks—especially attacks from the air, if not the ground. One of the most effective measures to protect these facilities would seem to be taking them out of harm's way, in particular, by placing them either underground or in bunker-style buildings with sloping walls that could deflect much of a truck bomb blast. The following discussion of this remedy relies heavily on a recent paper by representatives from the Defense Threat Reduction Agency, James Madison University, and the Board on Infrastructure and the Constructed Environment, National Research Council, which discusses the relevance of underground facilities for physical protection of critical infrastructure.[12] Other material is drawn from a National Academy Press report, also on the use of underground facilities, issued in 1998.[13]

The first of these reports states the advantages of underground facilities (UGFs):

> The physical protection provided by UGFs is superlative. They can be built to withstand effects from essentially any explosive device including nuclear weapons. Their physical security benefits make them particularly well suited to ensuring the continuity and reconstitution of critical infrastructure functions. Dollar for dollar, underground construction provides higher levels of physical protection than similarly sized hardened above-ground structures since specially designed facade treatments, interior wall reinforcement and blast-resistant window glazing are not needed. . . . Although UGFs do not provide direct protection against cyber attacks, their physical strength makes them a safe haven for critical backup media crucial for recovery following a cyber attack.[14]

The paper goes on to cite extensive Norwegian experience with building underground facilities for critical infrastructures and a cost-benefit study by the Defense Threat Reduction Agency in 1999.[15] These studies indicate that initial construction costs for underground facilities may be higher but that total life-cycle costs are comparable to those for above-ground facilities. The cost benefits of underground facilities increase with size and with the need for higher levels of hardening of above-ground facilities.

A compromise design for minimizing blast effects on above-ground facilities seems possible, but this author has not been able to find relevant literature on the topic. It would seem that earth berms slanted at a 45-degree angle against the walls will deflect a truck bomb blast upward and away from the facility. However, one must consider how to protect entry doors and loading dock areas and perform engineering analyses to gauge the required thickness, slope, and other key parameters.

Physical Replication or Redundancy

Replicating a key processing center or node so it mirrors all transactions to and from the primary site is a standard method for achieving resiliency within critical information infrastructures. This type of duplication is common practice among main stock exchanges, major banks, and other similar institutions. Two main problems underlie this strategy: (1) It is expensive, requiring resources similar in scale to those of the primary site (or sites), and (2) if an attacker is already capable of planning simultaneous physical attacks, then the duplicate site merely becomes another hit on his list of nodes to be "taken out" in a coordinated operation. It is unlikely that an organization can keep the existence and location of such a major processing site secret enough for it to remain unavailable as a target.

Grid Computing, Peer-to-Peer Computing, Internet Architecture

Although underground "bunker" facilities and physical replication are obvious approaches to information infrastructure security, a third option, intriguing in its possibilities, has the potential to become available. It involves the emerging concept of "grid computing" as well as the associated concepts of peer-to-peer (P2P) systems and the inherently redundant and resilient architecture of the Internet itself.

Current discussion is speculative and based loosely on the following assumptions and definitions:

- The Internet is the most resilient worldwide communication system in existence.[16] It is also one of the most flexible, passing packets of bits representing anything—it knows or cares not what—from site to site or broadcasting them to multiple sites. These qualities make it a highly useful backbone both for communication and for distributed computation.
- Peer-to-peer systems allow files to be stored as redundant fragments in multiple nodes within a network, so subsets of them can

suffice for reconstituting the whole file and allow computations to be fragmented into parts; they also enable shared workspaces whose connections do not require a centralized file and coordination site.[16]

- Grid computing ties the above two concepts together into a total distributed computation system, no one node of which is critical to an operation. (One or more sites may be coordinating the process, or not.) Commercial offerings from Sun Microsystems and other vendors are fleshing out the grid computing concept with specific hardware and software solutions.
- Increasingly, critical information infrastructures are constructed from common "building blocks"—PCs, IP-based networks with routers and switches, file servers, and so forth. This type of construction enables processes to migrate as needed from the execution of programs residing at one physical site to another while accessing data and communications facilities available to all relevant sites by means of the common network.[17]

Examples of potentially relevant technologies in building a truly distributed information system include the following:[17]

- Publius, developed by researchers at AT&T Laboratories and New York University, is a system in which a document's content is encrypted and split into fragments that are then distributed randomly among participating servers. No central index exists. Only a few fragments are needed to reconstruct and decrypt it.
- Freenet, designed by Ian Clarke in 1999, is an unbrokered (i.e., no central controlling node) architecture in which each user's computer stores the content files it has handled most recently and responds to requests for those files. All content is encrypted.
- Groove Networks, founded by Lotus Notes developer Ray Ozzie, provides a secure collaborative workspace for subscribers, including communication tools (voice, instant messaging, text-based chat, threaded discussion), content-sharing tools (shared files), and joint-activity tools (co-Web browsing, multiple-user editing, group calendar). An organization's files and processing within a Groove environment is truly P2P, without any central controlling or coordinating node that could become a single point of failure.

Given the above technologies and trends, how might the processing in a key physical center be made truly redundant so a physical attack that severely damages the site does not significantly disrupt the critical information system for which it is an important node? A plausible speculation is that a site sending messages or transactions would mirror them by means of the network to multiple other sites on the Net so they are received redundantly. Each of the multiple sites is capable of processing the transaction or message, perhaps accessing one or more databases distributed among the sites in the process. Negotiations among the sites resolve which site (or sites) handle the processing, but if any one of them goes "dark," others can take over its role. All communications among sites are by means of the Internet itself or an IP-based network replicating its redundancy of links between nodes. (The assumption is that IP packets transiting open networks such as the Internet would be encrypted for security during this transit.)

Perhaps the greatest potential for disruption in the above sketch is with the often singular network links tying any node into the net. A link from a local node uses a telecommunication line to access a gateway hub into the larger network and, most often, a single such line runs from an office or processing center to the nearest telecom provider central office (CO) or Internet service provider (ISP) facility. Elsewhere, the author discusses options for redundancy within a "neighborhood" of critical facilities to reach backbone facilities for both power and telecommunications.[18]

The raw materials for fundamentally more distributed computing and file storage are becoming available from vendors, and they should be investigated for possible solutions to the major threat to critical information infrastructures posed especially by physical, kinetic attacks—ones that can disable key centers and nodes, perhaps simultaneously, for weeks or months.

Conclusions and Recommendations

Clearly, physical, kinetic (e.g., blast) effects can be created from easy-to-acquire materials. They involve low technology but are highly effective. Critical information infrastructure sites must be protected from these effects.

Most truly critical information infrastructure sites have developed dual, mirrored, or backup processing facilities to avoid a "single point of failure" for the system. However, terrorists and other adversaries have demonstrated increasing capability for, and interest in, conducting simultaneous, coordinated attacks. Thus, dual facilities cannot be considered a true safeguard.

Especially in the era of the Web and powerful search engines, attempting to achieve security by obscurity as a way to protect redundant processing sites seems doomed to failure; too many clues become accessible. At minimum, redundancy should not be relied on as a primary security tactic.

Two of the most promising safety and security measures for protection are (1) underground facilities or semi-above-ground facilities that are protected from blast effects by berms or other devices and (2) the potential of "grid computing" and P2P techniques to provide truly distributed processing and file storage over an IP-based network with redundant links (e.g., the Internet itself). The first technique is practical today; the second one is speculative but appears to hold promise for the future.

Notes

[1] B. S. Wesbury, "The Economic Cost of Terrorism," 2002, available at <http://usinfo.state.gov/journals/itgic/0902/itge/gj02.htm>.

[2] Command, control, communications, computers, intelligence, surveillance, reconnaissance.

[3] This methodology is also discussed in C. Pfleeger and S. L. Pfleeger, *Security in Computing*, 3d ed. (New York: Prentice Hall, 2003).

[4] Office of Energy Assurance, U.S. Department of Energy, *Vulnerability Assessment and Survey Program: Lessons Learned and Best Practices* (Washington, D.C.: U.S. Department of Energy, Sept 28, 2001), available at <http://oea.dis.anl.gov/documents.htm>.

[5] Unpublished briefing by Kevin O'Brien, RAND Europe, derived from RAND Terrorism Chronology, accessible, in part, at <http://db.mipt.org>.

[6] See the BMO Web site at <http://www.c3i.osd.mil/biometrics/>.

[7] Secret Internet Protocol Router Network.

[8] Unclassified Internet Protocol Router Network.

[9] See <http://www.identix.com/products/pro_info_biologon.html>.

[10] For an introduction to the evaluation of biometric systems, see P. J. Phillips, A. Martin, C. L. Wilson, and M. Przybocki, "An Introduction to Evaluating Biometric Systems," *IEEE Computer* (February 2000).

[11] D. A. Linger, G. H. Baker, and R.G. Little, "Applications of Underground Structures for the Physical Protection of Critical Infrastructure." Presented at the North American Tunneling Conference 2002, May 18–22, 2002, Seattle, Washington. Available at <http://www.ceworld.org/.../Presentations/CriticalInfrastructure/Applications-of-Underground-Structures-for-the.cfm>.

[12] Commission on Engineering and Technical Systems, *Use of Underground Facilities to Protect Critical Infrastructures* (Washington, D.C.: National Academies Press, 1998).

[13] Linger et al., "Applications of Underground Structures," 3–4.

[14] F. Gertcher, *Benefits and Costs of Protecting Infrastructure Systems Against Terrorist and Related Threats: Cost Analysis*, Report RT-0103-99 (Washington, D.C.: Defense Threat Reduction Agency, 1999).

[15] For a discussion of the robustness of the Internet in the immediate aftermath of September 11, 2001, see Computer Science and Telecommunications Board, *The Internet Under Crisis Conditions: Learning From September 11* (Washington D.C.: The National Academies Press, 2003).

[16] For an overview of P2P concepts, see Andy Oram, editor, *Peer-to-Peer: Harnessing the Benefits of a Disruptive Technology* (Sebastopol, CA: O'Reilly Media, 2001).

[17] These brief descriptions are excerpted from an unpublished 2001 RAND monograph by R. H. Anderson and W. Baer.

[18] E. Balkovich and R. H. Anderson, *Helping Neighborhoods Fend for Themselves: Toward Affordable Redundancy in the 'Last Mile' of Power and Telecommunication Networks* (Santa Monica, CA: RAND, 2003).

Chapter 3

Physical Vulnerabilities Exposed at the National Training Center

John D. Rosenberger

The following is an excerpt from a speech that was given by COL John Rosenberger, USA, at the annual U.S. Marine Corps Command and Control Symposium at Quantico, Virginia, in May 2000. He was the Chief of Staff of the 1st Cavalry Division at Fort Hood and the Commander of the 11th Armored Cavalry Regiment (ACR). The 11th ACR performs the mission of the Opposing Force (OPFOR) by acting as aggressors against U.S. Marine and Army units often equipped with the very latest in advanced technologies who build up, train, and maneuver at the National Training Center (NTC) at Fort Irwin.

To the 2,500 troopers of the 11th Armored Cavalry Regiment who make up the Opposing Force (OPFOR) at the U.S. Army's National Training Center (NTC), it came as no surprise to watch the 3rd Serbian Army march back into Serbia virtually unscathed by the relentless attacks of Global air power during the Kosovo conflict. It also came as no surprise to see the Serbian Army employ a wide variety of physical and electronic deception techniques, remain tactically well dispersed, and hide their combat systems in the infrastructure of cities and villages to preserve their combat power. Such tactics are old news to the combined arms team of the NTC OPFOR. The same strategies used by the Serbian Army have been learned and employed successfully by the OPFOR at the NTC since 1994—adaptive countermeasures critical to preserving combat capability at the tactical level of war against the impressive array of intelligence collection and attack technologies employed by America's joint team. This example is only one of several insights the OPFOR can provide into the limitations and vulnerabilities of current war fighting technology that underpins America's style of warfare in the 21st century. All of these insights and lessons learned are directly relevant to the pending combat operations in Iraq.

In the past 10 years, NTC OPFOR has exposed many limitations and vulnerabilities inherent to the war fighting technologies U.S. joint services are currently pursuing. Moreover, they have learned to defeat them just like any adaptive and savvy opponent will do—exactly as the Serbian Army did awhile back. These exposed vulnerabilities are compelling on several fronts, not simply to ensure we make smarter technological investments in the years ahead but, equally important, to ensure that we do not forfeit combat effectiveness, the ability to deter, or the ability to quickly defeat our enemies at both the operational and tactical levels of war. As a start, we at NTC have learned that active and passive force protection measures are vital to preserving combat power against asymmetric technologies—asymmetric, in this case, meaning some technological capability that provides a decisive advantage over an opponent in combat. For example, cruise missiles, laser-guided bombs, satellite reconnaissance systems, high-altitude reconnaissance aircraft, and unmanned aerial vehicles have provided the United States an asymmetric combat advantage over all opponents in the past decade. In response to these capabilities, opposing forces, at least at NTC, have learned that thermal deception, vehicle and unit dispersion, decoys of all types, camouflage, concealment, and electronic deception are vital means and ways to protect and preserve ground combat power.

Furthermore, the OPFOR has learned that air power and overhead intelligence acquisition systems have significant limitations and are inherently vulnerable to deception—even in desert and mountainous terrain and, by extension, certainly so in densely forested areas and jungles, not to mention complex urban terrain. We have learned that if we limit our movement, do not create dust clouds, remain tactically dispersed, use camouflage, and employ decoy equipment, we will absorb few losses. The Serbian Army and paramilitary forces employed the same methodology of force protection in the dense forests, cities, and villages in Kosovo. By using a combination of these force protection techniques, the effectiveness of attacks against ground forces can be limited and thereby endured.

We have learned how to deceive the operators and analysts behind the intelligence acquisition screens and leverage them to set conditions for success. Techniques in offensive operations and infiltration can be used to create a weakness in the enemy's defense, permitting rapid penetration and exploitation. Employment of these techniques set conditions for OPFOR tactical success several times in the past. The Serbs used similar techniques to preclude effective air attacks against their ground combat forces and deceive NATO forces about their actual strength, disposition, and location. Even more ingenious, the Serbs used appreciation of this vulnerability to lure NATO attack aircraft into attacking organized columns of civilian vehicles, then exploiting the scenes of carnage via the international media. Such a strategy, designed to attack the solidarity of the NATO coalition, is an extreme example of information warfare. In short, against a savvy opponent, acquisition systems have little intelligence value to tactical and operational commanders unless the data or images are confirmed quickly by another real-time imagery system or a well-trained reconnaissance team with the capability and optical resolution to discern the exact composition and types of vehicles acquired.

Another important lesson we have learned is that the key to defeating forces equipped with sophisticated collection, targeting, and situational awareness technologies is to gain information dominance quickly in the initial phase of the operation. If we can disrupt the enemy's ability to move information across the battlefield, then we can quickly level the playing field and negate the asymmetric advantage.

The location of stationary and relatively immobile communication node centers is easy to predict, given a line-of-sight analysis within an area of operations. There are a limited number of accessible positions where comprehensive line-of-sight communications can be established and sustained. Accordingly, the OPFOR tasks both its division and regimental reconnaissance teams to find these large, easily identifiable communication sites during the reconnaissance phase of an operation. Once found, and they always are, we attack the sites with accurate long-range artillery, rockets, or fixed-wing assets during the first phase of offensive or defensive operations. This strategy stops the flow of digits, quickly levels the playing field, and eliminates the asymmetric advantage afforded by the technology.

Line-of-sight technologies are easily disrupted by hills and mountainous terrain, unless continually supported by multiple aerial or ground retransmission stations positioned within the brigade's area of operations. Furthermore, this type of technology is even more limited, if not ineffective, when fighting in cities, a lesson painfully learned by the Russians in Groznyy, Chechnya, in 1996 and again this past year. While the Russians struggled to maintain FM communications to control operations, the Chechens used cellular telephones and commercial satellite communications to coordinate their defensive operations within the city.

In summation, from the experience from the OPFOR and the study of actual battlefield maneuvers, we have learned that there is no substitute for well-trained ground reconnaissance teams in war fighting at the tactical level of war. Despite all the intelligence and information technology provided to brigade task force commanders over the past 6 years, the OPFOR regimental commanders, using 1960s–1970s technology and unaided by overhead reconnaissance systems, have always had better, near-perfect information about the strength, composition, location, and disposition of their opponents. Their opponents, on the other hand, have remained and continue to remain relatively blind, despite the bloom of technology. This ability to see the battlefield better than their opponents, despite the introduction of sophisticated technologies, is provided by our division and regimental reconnaissance teams, undoubtedly some of the best-trained tactical reconnaissance teams in the world.

The indisputable fact is that well-trained observers (reconnaissance teams) in sufficient number to establish observation throughout the depths of the battlefield and armed with effective, secure communication, easily offset the supposed asymmetric advantages of overhead reconnaissance platforms in the business of close combat at brigade level and below. Moreover, from a practical perspective, overhead reconnaissance platforms cannot classify a bridge and determine if it will support the movement of forces, find and determine feasible fording sites across rivers or streams, locate minefields or bypasses, or provide any accurate information about enemy strength and dispositions within cities, the most likely battlefields in our future.

In conclusion, if the insights provided cause you to question the direction, design, and investments we have made in trying to create information dominance at the tactical level of war, that is good. If these insights foster a change in your perspective about the practical value and utility of technology by exposing its limitations and vulnerabilities, that is good, too. If these same insights drive our joint team to pursue more prudent technological investments in the future or drive the creation of better organizations, equipment, doctrine, tactics, and techniques for employing technology in the future, then that is even better. If they convince you that we should keep teaching our soldiers, sailors, and Marines how to read a map and navigate with compass in hand and keep teaching artillerymen how to survey their firing positions and teach our staff personnel what to do when the screens go blank, that is icing on the cake.

Finally, if these arguments convince you that OPFOR at our combat training centers can provide critical insights into the limitations and vulnerabilities of technology, informing our judgment to ensure that the Department of Defense wisely adapts to and dominates threats in the 21st century, then my objective has been accomplished. One thing is for certain: If we ignore the lessons and successful countermeasures that our Opposing Force has made and continues to make against technology, then we ignore the work of these great soldiers at our peril.

Chapter 4

Dealing with Physical Vulnerabilities

Bruce W. MacDonald

Addressing the physical aspects of information system vulnerabilities is really nothing new. Military planners and practitioners have been worried about this problem for centuries and, probably, for millennia. In one of Julius Caesar's most successful campaigns during the war he waged in North Africa, the key to Caesar's battle victory at Alexandria in 48 B.C. was the creation and subsequent interception of a false written communication, a sealed papyrus document. Caesar had an aide write a seriously misleading letter purporting to be from the king of Pergamum to Caesar. Affixing the seal from another of that king's communications, he sent away the document in such a way that it was sure to be intercepted by his Egyptian enemies. The confusion that followed led to Caesar's victory.[1] Here, a physical intrusion into his enemy's communications system—not the destruction of the system—led to victory for Caesar. So it can be argued that the problem of information systems' physical vulnerability is at least 2,000 years old. The only difference today is that some of the tools and methods involved have become more advanced.

The Growing Potential of Disproportionate Effects

What is new in information systems' physical vulnerability is an increasing emphasis on nodal attacks that are capable of producing disproportionate effects. If we could destroy one system in an enemy's infrastructure, the results might be militarily interesting. But if we are able to find the key system of the whole infrastructure, then we can potentially hit the jackpot from a military perspective. However, finding the key system usually requires substantial planning and analysis.

We have had examples of this strategy in peacetime and in war. In July 2001, a train carrying chemicals and paper products derailed in a downtown Baltimore tunnel, caught fire, and, in the ensuing 5 days, caused a series of infrastructure failures and public safety problems. The train leaked several thousand gallons of hydrochloric acid into the tunnel, and the fire caused a water main to burst. More than 70 million gallons of water spread over the downtown area, flooding buildings and streets and leaving downtown businesses without water. The fire also burned through fiber-optic cables, causing widespread telecommunication problems, while the fire and burst water main damaged power cables and left 1,200 Baltimore buildings without electricity. Similar events are certainly also possible in military settings.[2]

One classic wartime example is the effect that Allied bombing of German ball bearing plants had on the German war machine in World War II. Had the Allies kept up the bombing, the failures in ball bearing production would have quickly spread to much larger failures in Germany's capabilities.[3] According to Albert Speer, Hitler's Minister of Armaments and War Production, "had they continued the attacks of March and April [1944] with the same energy, we would quickly have been at our last gasp."[4]

In chapter 3, Army Colonel John Rosenberger, who headed up the opposing forces at the National Training Center, outlines the steps the opposing forces he commanded took in their training sessions to defeat the best forces in the United States. Rosenberger points out the ways in which targeted, intelligent, and timely physical attacks, as well as other attacks, can reduce or negate the effectiveness of U.S. battlefield information systems on which our armed forces now highly depend and will increasingly depend in the future. The lesson is clear: We must address not only physical but also cyber vulnerabilities in our military information systems.

Current battlefield information systems offer U.S. forces greatly enhanced capabilities. However, although they make great servants, they can be bad masters. We need to consider them as adjuncts to the main task at hand and not overly rely on them to work at all times. The Rosenberger analysis is a timely reminder that, in our rush to strengthen information assurance through cyber means, we must not forget the physical dimensions of the systems. His analysis does not mean that we need to choose between cyber and physical elements; we need to consider both. In many ways, the line between physical and cyber attacks to defeat or disrupt military information systems already is blurred.

Physical means can be used to insert cyber agents into information systems, leading to cyber attacks. For example, a chip-scale transmitting device can be inserted into a hostile PC or signal processor, and useful information can be exfiltrated by a variety of means. The insertion is physical insertion, but the extraction is cyber-based information. In addition, cyber attacks can be used to create physical damage in systems and even to destroy them. Sometimes, a cyber attack can cause network systems physically to shut down or overheat. Examples of this strategy are classified out of necessity, but they make interesting case studies. A sophisticated cyber attacker against U.S. forces will want to achieve key military objectives. As a result, he is not after destruction as much as he is after certain effects, and he will use whatever means he can—physical, cyber, or other—to meet his goals. Our enemies very well may be cleverer than we sometimes give them credit for being. We should never make the mistake of thinking they are stupid, even though from time to time they will behave that way. From a defender's perspective, or the perspective of a battlefield commander, the issue becomes how to manage vulnerability and risk across the board, where we define risk as any threat to mission success.

No substitute exists for a rigorous, end-to-end nodal analysis and overall risk assessment of our information systems, leading ultimately to a review of the entire defense information infrastructure in its largest sense. But given the increasing level of connectedness that the Department of Defense (DOD) now has and the vastly increased levels planned for the future, we now may see where an incident or attack in one part of the country might affect others in a large theater of operations. If an opponent were to take out the right node in one place, its destruction not only could affect battle operations in the immediate proximity but also might spread elsewhere throughout the theater with unknown ramifications. Until very recently, interconnectivity such as described here was not the case, but it likely will continue to increase as weapons become more and more dependent on what we now call the Global Information Grid (GIG). Considering this trend and looking at the requirement for end-to-end nodal analysis, we are not doing as good a job as we should be. Often, the software on which our information systems run is not sufficiently verified and validated. And we do even less for the larger information systems in which the software operates.

Nodal analyses and vulnerability assessment are key aspects of the physical vulnerability issue. They are crucially important to military readiness and cannot be delegated to people who have a vested interest in the outcome of the assessments. Program managers and commanders have too big a stake in assessment results to be left with the responsibility to perform these tasks themselves. Some combination of players is needed, perhaps coming from the Joint Program Office (Special Technical Measures) in Dahlgren or from the Office of the Secretary of Defense (OSD) Test and Evaluation office or from some other outside entity with the resources to do it. If the assessments are not outsourced, then we run the risk of receiving glowing reports in peacetime, only to find out later that our enemies (who perhaps because of inside information gained by a variety of means) are able to find key nodal points and cause substantial damage to force capabilities that had been believed to be protected.

In performing these assessments, analysts need to look at the possibility of the failure of different components in the information system along with the possibility of failure caused by downstream consequences of other attacks. This class of issues raises the question of interdependency. Destroying a key stockpile of consumables such as fuel that runs generators that power remotely deployed systems on which an information system critically depends can take that system out as assuredly as a direct physical attack on the system itself. In fact, an attack on consumables may be even more potent because, if the consumables are not there, then the system cannot be reconstituted or returned to action in a timely manner.

Physical vulnerability of critical U.S. information systems is more than a "guns, guards, gates, and firewall" exercise. Sophisticated risk assessment must consider vulnerabilities for specific assets more broadly than traditionally has been the case. One aspect of this kind of assessment involves thinking about threats or vulnerabilities. Two of the biggest threats we face are Murphy's Law and Mother Nature. Large complex information infrastructures are going to repeatedly be subjected to unintentional physical assaults of all sorts from time to time, probably more so under the stress of combat operations. We would be foolish to ignore these threats, which will become more complex and more involved as the GIG shapes up and additional information system hardware is added to it. Furthermore, these potential disruptions have the silver lining of providing insight to system designers and those responsible for the reliable functioning of information systems.

One aspect of this challenge is information "hyperload." At present, we certainly have large amounts of information to deal with, protect, and assure, but this current challenge will pale in comparison to what we will face in the next few years. The problem will not increase by only a factor of two or three. If trends continue, the problem will be exponentially greater than what we face today—thousands, even millions of times more severe. Unless quantum computing becomes a reality very soon, a major problem will blossom. Agencies such as the National Imagery and Mapping Agency (NIMA) and Defense Intelligence Agency (DIA) have already been told that improving the Processing, Exploitation, Dissemination System

(PEDS) is a top priority. Congress has already expressed its displeasure on this subject and is likely to continue to do so.

One area in which much work is being conducted involves microsensors; soon, we will have an extremely large number of sensors providing information to be managed, synthesized, transmitted, and brought to commanders' attention.[5] This major increase in information will also present a major increase in opportunities for physical disruption. One appealing aspect of the microsensor approach, of course, is that it addresses some of the concerns about concentrating information in only a few major nodes. The microsensor approach provides a finer-grained picture of the battlefield or other areas of interest, which is clearly desirable. From a security perspective, however, the advent of microsensors is a two-edged sword. The obvious benefit is that microsensors will decentralize and spread out information rather than allow us to rely on one big sensor node, which makes a very attractive target for physical attack. In this way, they offer a means by which to reduce the profile of any one component in the system. Seeking this type of sensor decentralization is common sense, of course. However, one drawback is the potential for a microsensor system to offer a profusion of entry points for hostile forces to access the sensor system. Likewise, Air Force plans for new airborne sensor platforms such as the Multisensor Command and Control Aircraft (MC2A)[6] and multispectral-hyperspectral UAVs) will further add to the information onslaught.[7]

The 2000 Defense Science Board's Defensive Information Operations Task Force (DIOTF) pointed out that Joint Vision 2020 envisions future warfighting plans as increasingly dependent on a vast information backbone, the GIG.[8] As the task force pointed out, in many ways, we are betting the farm on this infrastructure. As a result, although it generally is not considered as a weapon system, this Global Information Grid will be one of the most important major weapon systems in the U.S. arsenal—and will need to be treated as such.[9]

The overwhelming majority of the GIG infrastructure will depend on commercial infrastructures over which DOD will not have much, if any, control. And much of that GIG infrastructure will be accessible to adversaries.[10] At some point, this dependence will create important tensions. One of the ironies is that, although we want to use the GIG to focus exclusively on military operations, more and more of the physical hardware and infrastructure will be non-military. DOD depends on available commercial telecommunications services for most of its communications needs for cost reasons. Growing trends like this one are prevalent throughout the Defense Department. Civilians, even contractors, perform key services for DOD on a regular basis, even in Operations. DOD, whether we like it or not, is depending increasingly on commercial infrastructures of all sorts, and the implications for physical infrastructure security are huge. This trend likely will continue to increase and along with it, the security implications.

In 1960, 70 percent of the U.S. electronics market was the Department of Defense. Today, DOD makes up about 2 percent at best, and the percentage is dropping.[11] This trend means that 40 years ago, DOD basically dominated the electronics field; now, new directions in electronics are largely at the mercy of the commercial electronics business, over which DOD has little control. Today, defense electronics technology heavily depends on what is happening in the commercial world. So DOD is often forced to use commercial offerings as best it can and accept the opportunities for attacks. This condition is true for electricity systems, water systems, and all those other infrastructures on which DOD depends.

As a result, a tension exists, quite frankly, where we have militarily unique physical aspects of these infrastructures. In other words, defense wants especially good security and can secure its own unique components, but it still depends on commercial equipment, which by its very nature may not be as secure. In addition, commercial civilian infrastructures present their own problems. This growing interconnectedness with civilian infrastructures holds not only great opportunity but also avenues for vulnerability. OSD recognizes this problem and sees a variety of management and security tools that can address this problem. They identify the Global Grid Security Approach as using many encryption links per unit (including new technologies such as the Fastlane encryptor), lower aggregated device costs, more efficient management, and scaleable security protection. New technologies include smart cards and a vast array of possible biometric devices and techniques.

However, even strict biometric safeguards and their information components could be overcome if military personnel are captured. Biometric safeguards are very important, and their increasing use is encouraging. However, biometric safeguards will impose operational constraints that need to be addressed. We do not have to address the scenario we saw in the movie "Minority Report," where eyeballs of dead or not-so-dead people can be implanted, but the movie plot is nevertheless a cautionary tale. Even subtler than the outright capture or destruction of information system components would be the physical emplacement of devices in the components. Particularly in a pre-war or pre-battle environment like the one we are in right now, this type of compromise could siphon off information or cause valuable information to be transmitted in a way that would have a low probability of interception. Certainly any equipment, if lost and later recovered, needs to be viewed with extreme suspicion before it is ever reintroduced into the battlefield.

Conclusions and Recommendations

The general point here is that physical attacks do not have to be destructive to be effective. Nondestructive attacks may be preferable in some ways because we would continue to use the compromised equipment whereas the destroyed equipment presumably would be replaced and the system recovered. In addition, physical attacks can also be used to channel an adversary into using other systems that can be more exploitable. The fundamental characteristic behind most physical failure modes is the presence of key nodes without which the system either cannot function or cannot function well. This vulnerability suggests a growing need to have decentralized information systems that can function even in a degraded condition, exhibiting graceful degradation, resiliency, and self-healing.

Another important point is reconstitutability. Often, the focus when looking at system vulnerabilities is on avoiding attack, destruction, or compromise, all of which are certainly important. However, we also need to look at how easily a system can be reconstituted as a key aspect of survivability and assurance. Eventually, these systems are going to be damaged or compromised in some way; that is the nature of the battlefield. We need to look at (a) knowing when a system has been compromised and (b) being able to recover from it. The Federal Interagency Working Group on Critical Infrastructure Protection R&D identified reconstitutability as a key area needing further attention and analytical research.[12]

From a physical perspective, decentralized, resilient information system components are probably one of the best counters to physical threats, not to mention cyber threats, that we could have. The World Wide Web is a good example of this type of system, but it needs physical emulation to allow this kind of analysis. End-to-end evaluation of information systems by outsiders from a physical and cyber standpoint as well as red team analyses are critical to ensuring a robust DOD information infrastructure. At the same time, these decentralized, resilient systems will pose a greater challenge to update for information security and to guard against compromise.

For a long time, we focused primarily on the physical side of infrastructure protection; recently, we have experienced a rush into cyber protection. Although the cyber dimension of assurance is critically important, we need to remember that physical ways to compromise our systems also must be taken into account. The Defense Science Board's Defensive Information Operations Task Force in 2000 reported a need for more robust red team analyses, more consideration of the kind of defensive analytical work done by the Joint Program Office, and more rigorous examination for our systems.

We also need readiness metrics, which raises the whole question about readiness of our information systems against physical and cyber threats. These readiness measures have to be strengthened and viewed as being at least as important as more traditional measures of military readiness. Better modeling and field testing are also needed to determine infrastructure vulnerability. We do not want to become a slave to computer modeling, certainly, but it may be the safest way to uncover the interdependencies and subtle vulnerabilities that threaten our defensive information infrastructure.

The increasing information dependence of our military force structure is the proper way forward, but we must remember that, in the commercial world, security is too often an afterthought. One of the important factors from a DOD planning perspective is that, from the very start, DOD knows and expects its systems to be attacked. Yet to hear an outside voice saying that DOD is not defending its systems properly is always difficult and, often, unwelcome. Thus, it is tremendously important that we give more power and authority to those parts of DOD capable of providing independent analyses, red team analyses, and the like to make recommendations for additional steps to improve the physical and other dimensions of information systems security.

Notes

[1] As recounted in Colleen McCullough, *The October Horse* (New York: Simon & Schuster, 2002).

[2] James P. Peerenboom, Ronald E. Fisher, Steven M. Rinaldi, and Terrance K. Kelly, "Studying the Chain Reaction," a paper presented at Electric Perspectives, Edison Electric Institute, January–February 2002.

[3] Albert Speer, *Inside the Third Reich: Memoirs* (New York: Macmillan, 1970), 286.

[4] Ibid.

[5] See, for example, DARPA's R&D in this area and the Defense Microelectronics Activity's Microsensor Systems Program. The Army's Night Visions Laboratory is also starting up a program in this area.

[6] "Air Force Set to Release RFP for M2CA Program," *Aerospace Daily*, November 8, 2002. Private communications with Air Force Research Lab/Sensors Directorate Personnel, 2002.

[7] Private communications with Air Force Research Lab/Sensors Directorate Personnel, 2002.

[8] Defensive Information Operations Task Force, "Protecting the Homeland," Report of the Defense Science Board 2000 Summer Study, Executive Summary, Volume I (Washington, D.C.: Department of Defense, 2001), 12.

[9] Ibid. See also, "The GIG is a Weapon System," in "Protecting the Homeland," Volume II, Part 2, Annexes, 41.

[10] "Global Grid," a briefing to the Defense Science Board Task Force on Defensive Information Operations, July 17, 2000.

[11] Conversation with Dr. Al Joseph, former senior scientist, Rockwell Science Center, and founder and former chairman of the board, Vitesse Semiconductor, Inc.

[12] Critical Infrastructure Protection R&D Interagency Working Group, "Report on the Federal Agenda in Critical Infrastructure Protection Research and Development: Research Vision, Objectives, and Programs" (Washington, D.C.: White House Office of Science and Technology Policy, January 2001), 32.

Chapter 5

Vulnerabilities to Electromagnetic Attack of Defense Information Systems

John M. "Mike" Borky

The critical and growing importance of information dominance to the effectiveness of U.S. and allied military operations is well established.[1] Such dominance must be achieved through an information infrastructure that delivers robust, secure, timely, and efficient information services to commanders and warfighters at all echelons of a force and at all levels of conflict. That much is clear, but behind that glib string of adjectives—robust, secure, timely, efficient—lies a thicket of complex issues, many of which are poorly understood by those responsible for developing doctrine and tactics and for specifying and acquiring the assets used to implement them. Many factors, including both physical effects in the battlespace and operational constraints on rapid, synchronized actions, combine to determine the speed, precision, and correctness with which information is used to achieve desired effects.

The most important concern is that, by committing so heavily to information technology as a key enabler of decisive, effects-based operations, the U.S. military has made itself vulnerable to attack on inadequately protected systems, especially by less sophisticated opponents. This is a classic issue of asymmetrical warfare, and has been highlighted by study after study.[2] The emphasis to date has been largely on physical attacks, such as sabotage or direct attacks on key information nodes, and on cyber attacks, such as hacking and injection of software viruses. However, to these must be added the susceptibility of friendly information systems and networks to disruption or damage by electromagnetic (EM) weapons.[3]

At a high level, the problem looks fairly simple. A typical scenario involves the use of a high power radio frequency (HPRF) or high power microwave (HPM) device against a target such as a network of computers and telecommunications equipment. The attacker injects one or more bursts of energy into the target system by irradiating it with an antenna or by directly coupling to power or signal lines. The resulting electrical transient, if it reaches sensitive electronics, can disrupt the target's operations, corrupt its content, or even physically damage its components. Anyone who has suffered a computer freeze-up after a static electric shock or had a computer damaged by a lightning strike has an intuitive sense of the risks posed by transient pulses of electrical energy.

However, the large number of EM devices that are candidates for creating such weaponry, and the even greater disparity in the characteristics of electronic systems that determine their EM susceptibility, make the analysis of such attacks very difficult. In addition to the scenario just sketched, EM attacks may involve high-power lasers to blind electro-optical (EO) sensors and communications equipment or to damage target structures. Still other options include traditional electronic warfare (EW) techniques such as jamming and deception, and even the use of nuclear weapons to generate an electromagnetic pulse (EMP) event that could cause widespread destruction of electronic and electrical power systems. Relevant data on EM weapons and target effects is frequently classified.

Accordingly, the objective of this chapter is to frame the overall EM attack problem and, using representative values for weapon and target parameters, to develop a sense of the seriousness of this threat to current and future military systems and operations. The focus is on the operational level of warfare; hence, the concentration will be on the impacts of EM attack on theater-level command and control (C2) processes. We will first briefly summarize the general categories of EM weapons and effects. The majority of the chapter will then consider the threat most likely to be encountered, namely the use of HPRF/ HPM weapons to disrupt C2 systems, and will illustrate the complexity of determining both the susceptibility of target systems and the required characteristics of effective weapons. Finally, we will offer some recommendations on ways to protect information systems against EM attack and thus minimize the ability of such weapons to deny friendly forces the operational advantages of information dominance.

Fundamentals of Electromagnetic Attack Systems

A discussion of the Fundamentals of electromagnetic attack systems must address three areas: categories, effects, and mechanisms.

Categories of EM Attack

Any use of EM energy, from RF to X-rays, to interfere with an opponent's electronic assets is a mode of EM attack, but physics limits the number of EM devices that are practical as weapons. The following are some categories of EM attack that are of concern:

High Energy Lasers (HELs)

As systems like the Airborne Laser (ABL) approach operational status, the use of HELs as true tactical weapons is becoming a reality. There have been reports of vision damage to human eyes caused by even the modest output power of laser range finders. EO systems used for both sensing (e.g., forward-looking infrared (FLIR) imaging systems) and communications (e.g., broadband data links) are susceptible to jamming and possibly damage if lased through their optics. Ultimately, HELs will be used as speed-of-light weapons to burn through or otherwise damage target structures or to ignite fuel or explosives. Counters to such threats range from sophisticated techniques for hardening optical systems to the brute force approach of attacking the HEL platform using whatever weapons are available. In terms of the subject of this chapter, HELs can be thought of as simply a new category of weapon that might be used to damage or destroy the nodes and links of a network, e.g., by shooting down an airborne relay platform. Fortunately, it will be some time before long-range HEL weapons are small or light enough to be agile or easily concealed. Yet they must be accounted for in intelligence gathering and operational planning, protected against in system design, and counterattacked if they appear in the battle space.

Electromagnetic Pulse

It has been known for decades that a nuclear burst produces an intense pulse of EM energy, and analysts predict that an EMP event could produce very widespread damage to electrical power grids, telecommunications networks, and other unprotected systems. Models have shown that a tactical nuclear warhead detonated in space would, in addition to destroying nearby satellites immediately, "pump" the Van Allen belts and thereby cause the death of any non-nuclear hardened satellites in a matter of days to weeks. Given concerns over such weapons falling into the hands of terrorists or rogue states, the threat of an EM attack must be considered as both real and potentially powerfully destructive. The primary effect on military capabilities would come about through the destruction of civilian infrastructure used for power, communications, transportation, and other support. However, such a strike, by definition, would take conflict out of the realm of conventional warfare. Disruption of theater C2 systems would require emergency measures to ensure the survival of vital national centers and massive strategic retaliation.

Electronic Warfare

A much more likely EM threat is posed by widely available systems used to jam or deceive RF and EO sensors and communications. EO jammers to defeat missile guidance systems are being developed for aircraft protection. The pointing and tracking problems involved in jamming a sensor or optical communications link mean that this threat probably is limited to momentary outages of specific nodes or assets, rather than broad disruption of information processes. RF EW systems will be taken as defining the low end of the RF weapon energy spectrum and treated accordingly in the analysis that follows.

High Power RF/High Power Microwave Weapons

HRPF/HPM systems round out the inventory of feasible EM attack options and are the primary focus of the remainder of this chapter. Many observers have speculated that such weapons are highly developed and may be near operational deployment.[4] They can use a wide assortment of thermionic (vacuum tube), spark gap, solid state, and other EM sources and can operate at various frequencies, bandwidths, power levels, and pulse shapes, depending on the nature of the source used, the platform that carries the weapon, and the targets to be attacked. Most such weapon concepts involve radiating one or more pulses of EM energy through some kind of antenna with the beam pointed at the target.

Effects of EM Attack

The next area that must be addressed is the range of effects EM attacks can cause in a target system. Based on the previous discussion, we will restrict ourselves to RF weapons and their effects. A great many such effects are possible, depending on the nature of the target system. For convenience, we will divide the subject into three broad system categories: sensors, communications, and computer networks, and will define a set of three effects levels for each. In each case there is an implicit fourth "No Effect" level, which does not mean evidence of an EM weapon being employed cannot be detected, but rather that the induced effects are too small to interfere with the proper functioning of the target.

Sensors

Here we include various kinds of radars, electronic or signal intelligence (ELINT/SIGINT) collectors, EO imaging systems, chemical/biological agent detectors, and any other systems that collect physical signatures about the battle space or environment. RF sensors may be attacked with EW jamming or deception. All sensors are potentially susceptible to disruption or damage of their electronics.

- Level 1 – Interference. The sensor is either jammed or deceived by EW or upset by induced transients such that it suffers effects like reduced range or sensitivity or loss of track (breaklock) on a tracked target. The sensor resumes normal functioning when the EM attack ceases.
- Level 2 – Disruption. The sensor is disabled or degraded and requires external intervention (e.g., an electronic reset) to resume normal operation.
- Level 3 – Damage. One or more components of the sensor system are damaged and must be repaired or replaced.

Communications

RF and EO communications systems can be attacked by EM weapons in exactly the same way as sensors. This category includes tactical radios and data links, satellite communication channels, and long haul communications such as troposcatter radios and microwave relays. Landline communications, whether fiber optic or wire cable, can be attacked via their transmission, reception, and relay electronics.

- Level 1 – Interference or Upset. An induced increase in noise or data errors degrades the quality of voice communications or significantly increases the bit error rate or dropped packet/message rate in digital communications. Communications return to normal when the EM attack ceases.
- Level 2 – Disruption. The communication channel is disabled or degraded and requires external intervention (e.g., an electronic reset) to resume normal operation.
- Level 3 – Damage. One or more components of the communication system are damaged and must be repaired or replaced.

Computer Networks

In this category we place individual computers, computers connected by a local area network (LAN) or equivalent, and associated equipment such as storage devices, printers, user workstations, and telecommunications equipment. Depending on their intensity, timing, duration, and point of entry, electrical transients induced by an EM attack can cause an assortment of effects. Individual computers or network interfaces can be frozen. Network messages can be corrupted or lost. Faulty data can be written to disks and existing data can be corrupted. At high enough levels, components can be damaged.

- Level 1 – Upset. One or more computers, network interfaces, or connected devices cease to operate correctly. Operation returns to normal when the EM attack ceases or requires only minor operator action (e.g., a warm boot or restarting an application program).
- Level 2 – Latchup or Shutdown. One or more computers, network interfaces, or connected devices cease to operate correctly ("crash") and require significant intervention (e.g., cycling power off and on or reloading software or data from backup media) to resume normal operation.
- Level 3 – Damage. One or more components of equipment connected to the network are damaged and must be repaired or replaced.

Mechanisms of EM Attack

We now turn to the phenomena through which an electronic attack is delivered. First, we briefly look at EW or, more generally, EM attacks using low power sources, followed by the use of HPRF/HPM weapons. This treatment of a highly complex situation is necessarily greatly simplified and includes only the level of mathematical analysis needed to reach the goal of an overall assessment of the EM attack threat. More rigorous and complete discussions can be found in the references.[5]

One useful simplification is to distinguish between "front door" and "back door" attacks. The former refers to attacking a system by injecting RF energy through the system's own RF hardware, usually the antenna and RF receiver, using the frequency band in which the target is designed to operate. The simplest idea is to overwhelm the signals, which the target system seeks to detect with electronic noise. At a greater level of sophistication, signals might be constructed to deceive the target. At high power levels, a front door attack may even seek to burn out sensitive RF components, although properly designed systems include protective devices such as limiters that make this very hard to achieve. Back door attacks, by contrast, seek to inject energy by coupling to any part of the target's structure or electronics that can provide a "port of entry"(POE).

Low Power EM Attack

EW and other low-power attacks are inherently front door techniques because they cannot overcome the poor efficiency with which back door POEs couple external energy into a target. The best known of these is simply noise jamming, bombarding the target with incoherent signals that saturate the receiver or mask the signals of interest. Deception techniques against RF sensors include range and velocity gate walk-off, false target injection, and many others. RF communications can also be jammed and, with some communications waveforms, it may be possible to modulate the jammer such that the target system perceives the false signal as real data coming at too high a rate to handle and thus to overload its internal buffers or to propagate "garbage" to other nodes of a network.

The susceptibility of sensors and communications to this kind of attack is well established. Generally, only Level 1 effects are produced. A sufficiently powerful or well-placed jammer will defeat an RF target, but design methods to reduce susceptibility are also well known. They include the use of high power transmitters to burn through jamming, high gain antennas and antennas that can point nulls (low gain regions) toward a jammer, sidelobe cancellers, and systems that use spread spectrum or frequency hopping waveforms to make ordinary narrowband jamming less effective. Ultimately, the best solution may be to reduce friendly system susceptibilities to the point where jammers become too expensive or too large and vulnerable to be practical weapons. A severe or sophisticated EW threat may require that resources be dedicated to finding and destroying the EM weapons being employed.

We will use two quick examples to illustrate this threat to theater information infrastructure. The first is an attempt by an opponent to deny friendly use of Global Positioning System (GPS) signals for platform navigation and weapon guidance. With current, relatively feeble GPS satellite power levels and unprotected GPS receivers, a noise jammer operating at the GPS frequencies with as little as 1-10 W of output power and built from easily available parts can prevent GPS reception at useful (to the opponent) ranges, e.g., to protect a high value target from GPS guided weapons. To counter this, friendly systems increasingly use interference rejecting antennas and receivers together with navigation systems that tightly couple a GPS receiver with an inertial navigation unit (INU). Loss of GPS, even for several minutes, can then be compensated for by the INU. In the long term, future GPS satellites will have higher power levels, including a high gain spot beam to greatly increase the available signal in an area of operations (AO). Once the required jammer power climbs to a kilowatt or more, as it will with these improvements, the jammer becomes a lucrative target that is easily located by its continuous RF emissions.

Another very real threat is the jamming of satellite communications (SATCOM). A fixed ground SATCOM station might have a 10 kW transmitter and a 60 dB gain antenna.[6] A jammer with enough effective radiated power (ERP) to overcome this signal would, again, be an expensive and attractive target. However, mobile SATCOM terminals on aircraft or vehicles necessarily have much less transmitter power and small antennas. A sophisticated opponent might well find it feasible and attractive to field effective jammers, especially since the locations of geostationary communication satellites are stationary and can be well known. Waveform design and frequency diversity may be helpful in reducing susceptibility but, once again, the operational solution is likely to be to treat these radiating threats as high priority targets, vulnerable to the same kinds of emitter location and precision strike systems used in the suppression of enemy air defenses (SEAD) campaigns. We will consider the impact of these low power EM attacks on theater C2 in a later section.

HPRF/HPM Attacks

To make the discussion of back door EM attacks with high power weapons tractable, we will decompose the end-to-end chain of events that starts with generation of the EM signal and ends with effects in the target as shown in figure 5–1. This technique is adapted from work by Dr. Carl Baum of the Air Force Research Laboratory.[7] Each stage in the engagement of a target by an HPRF/HPM weapon is characterized by its output. First, the RF source produces some output, often characterized as a power spectrum, i.e., output power as a function of frequency, $\mathbf{P_o(f)}$. This will be reduced by losses in the system so that the actual power available to be radiated is a slightly smaller transmitted power, $\mathbf{P_T(f)}$. Assuming this is radiated through a directional antenna, the ERP is the product of transmitter power and the antenna gain, also a function of frequency, $\mathbf{G_A(f)}$. The next stage is propagation of the energy to the target. In free space, the power drops off as one over the square of the range to the target.

Figure 5–1. **Stages in an HPRF/HPM Engagement**

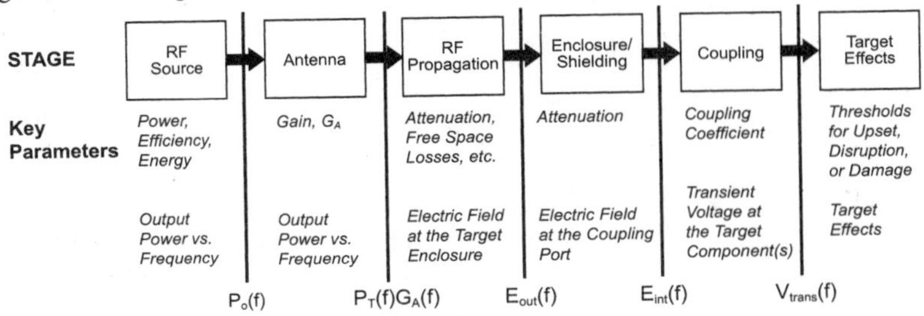

At high frequencies (above 10 GHz), atmospheric attenuation may further decrease the delivered energy. If there are intervening structures such as buildings, there may be further, frequency-dependent effects.

In any case, once the EM wave arrives at the target, it has some power spectrum or, equivalently, a frequency-dependent electric field intensity, $\mathbf{E_{out}(f)}$. The field is related to the original ERP and range by:

$$\frac{E_{out}(f)^2}{Z_s} = \frac{P_T(f)G_A(f)}{4\pi r^2},$$

where $\mathbf{r}$ is the range and $\mathbf{Z_s}$ is the impedance of free space (377 ohms). For generality, we assume the target is housed in a building, vehicle, or some other kind of enclosure that provides a measure of shielding, i.e., attenuation of the incoming weapon energy. This attenuation ranges from insignificant for a nonmetallic structure, like a residential house, to about 10 dB for a reinforced concrete wall to as much as 20/30 dB for an electrically bonded shelter or vehicle (acting as what is known technically as a Faraday cage). The energy that gets through structural shielding must now propagate through the target structure to one or more POEs on the victim electronics. Again, there may be frequency-dependent effects such as attenuation and wave guiding, and these will depend on the angle of arrival of the weapon energy on the structure. Eventually, an electric field, $\mathbf{E_{int}(f)}$, is present at the POE(s) where coupling to the actual electronics occurs. This coupling process, which can be thought of as equivalent to an antenna intercepting an EM wave and converting it to a voltage at the input to a radio receiver, is characterized by a coupling coefficient, often called an "effective height," and results in the actual transient voltage, $\mathbf{V_{trans}(f)}$, that is meant to produce adverse effects in the target.

The next obvious issue is the level of $\mathbf{V}_{\mathbf{trans}}$ required to cause Level 1, 2, or 3 effects, which we will call the effects threshold. There is no simple answer to estimating the value of the effects threshold in various targets, because it depends strongly on the nature of the electronics to be attacked. The relative hardness of a target to electronic attack depends on such factors as:

- whether the electronics involved use analog or digital circuitry
- the type and level of integration of individual components exposed to the induced transient
- whether the circuit incorporates protective design features such as differential wiring and surge protectors.

Figure 5–2. **Notional Example of End-to-End Analysis, Working Backward from Required Induced Transient Voltage to Estimated Source Parameters**

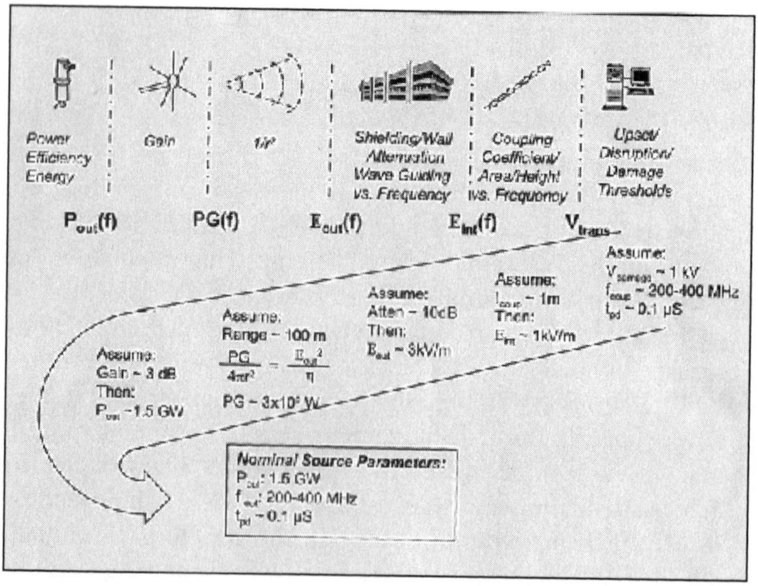

The effects threshold also depends on the width (time duration) of $\mathbf{V}_{\mathbf{trans}}$, which is likely to take the shape of an oscillating signal with decaying amplitude, called a damped sinusoid, as a result of coupling and circuit effects. At a given power level, a longer pulse deposits more energy into the component being attacked and thus increases the probability of effect, with the threshold decreasing roughly as the square root of the pulse duration. A source that is "rep rated," i.e., can deliver a train of pulses, may improve the chances of one or more pulses being delivered at favorable angles for good target coupling. As very rough guidelines, we will take 10 to 100 V as a typical Level 1 threshold, 50 to 500 V for Level 2, and 500 to 3,000 V for Level 3.

To put all this in some sort of perspective, figure 5–2 starts with a set of assumed but typical values for $\mathbf{V_{trans}}$ and works backward to an estimate of the required performance of an HPRF/HPM weapon. We assume first that a "hard kill," i.e., a Level 3 damage effect, is the required outcome of the engagement, and we take a 1 kV transient of 0.1 S duration as the required threshold values. We further assume that a UHF source operating in the frequency range of 200 to 400 MHz is best matched to the target enclosure and coupling structures. A coupling height, with dimensions of length, directly relates $\mathbf{E_{int}(f)}$ to $\mathbf{V_{trans}}$. It generally is on the order of the actual dimensions of a cable or cabinet slot that constitutes the POE. We take this for simplicity as 1 m, getting a value for $\mathbf{E_{int}(f)}$ of 1 kV/m; actual dimensions are typically in the range of 0.1–0.5 m. We next assume that the target enclosure shielding plus propagation losses inside amount to 10 dB in power or a factor of approximately 3 in voltage, so that $\mathbf{E_{out}(f)}$ is roughly 3 kV/m. Using the relation given earlier, this gives us an ERP at a range of 100 m on the order of 3 GW. Finally, assuming the weapon antenna gain is a modest 3 dB (a factor of two), reflecting the small size available on many delivery platforms, we get a required source output of 1.5 GW.

We will address the feasibility of such sources presently, but the point to be made here is that an HPRF/HPM attack is likely to be a short range proposition. If the tactical situation is such that a range of a kilometer is needed, still not exactly a standoff weapon, and all other parameters remain the same, the required source power goes up to 150 GW. Even if such a monster source could be built, it would run squarely up against another fundamental physical limitation known as air breakdown. At sea level, if the atmosphere is exposed to an RF energy density on the order of 800 kW/cm^2, it ionizes, much like a lightning discharge, and becomes a conductive plasma that severely attenuates the wave. To stay below this energy density, a 150 GW source would have to spread its output over an antenna of at least 2000m^2, or about the dimensions of a large transport aircraft.

Conversely, suppose that the desired effect is a Level 1 upset from a range of a kilometer. Now, with our assumed value for $\mathbf{V_{trans}}$ of 30 V, the required source power drops to 150 MW with a 3 dB antenna or to 30 MW if the antenna gain can be increased to 10 dB. At the assumed UHF frequency, this translates to an antenna size of about one square meter. These are much more attractive numbers from the viewpoint of implementing a source and antenna and integrating them with a delivery platform, whether a vehicle, a small aircraft (presumably unmanned), or a missile. Although these numbers are only ballpark estimates, they nevertheless give a first indication of what kinds of source powers are needed and what kinds of ranges and target effects are practical. In many situations, transient upsets are far more likely to be achieved than hard damage. Nevertheless, as we will see, these transient upsets may be enough to create serious consequences in the information systems and processes on which we are increasingly reliant.

Source Technology

One final technical matter must be addressed before we move on to the operational implications of EM attack. This is the state of the art in HPRF/HPM source technology, which will limit the kinds of sources available to an opponent wishing to use such weapons. For low power or EW weapons, not much can be said. This is a mature technology, and any combination of power, frequency coverage, modulation, and so forth required by a given technique can probably be provided, especially if this is seen as a stand-alone weapon where cost and efficiency are less important issues than would be the case in a purely EW application.

At the high power end, the picture is less clear. We are now talking about what is, effectively, an EM munition, and we have already alluded to the fact that a practical weapon must both deliver the output required to cause effects at acceptable ranges and be compatible with a delivery platform, a command and control scheme, and other practical considerations. The technology feasibility and issues associated with EM munitions have been examined over a period of many years in studies and experiments conducted by the Directed Energy Directorate of the Air Force Research Laboratory and other organizations. Much of the information presented in this paper was compiled in the course of these efforts.

In general, an HPRF/HPM system will include a prime power source (e.g., a battery), a device for converting prime power into the high pulsed power needed to drive the actual source (e.g., a pulse-forming network), the source (e.g., a microwave tube), some "plumbing" to connect the source output to an antenna, and the antenna itself. All of these together determine both the output of the EM weapon and its size, weight, cost, safety limitations, and platform compatibility. To cite only one of a host of issues, if the delivery platform is guided, its guidance system must be protected from the EM source, which will be operating at extremely close range and designed to wreak havoc on just such electronics.

The following are some of the important source characteristics that, in various combinations, create such a variety of alternatives for EM weapons.

- Bandwidth: RF and microwave sources are very loosely categorized as narrowband or broadband. While the definition varies, a typical narrowband source uses technology similar to that in other RF transmitters, such as a radar, and generates RF energy over a frequency range of from 2 or 3 up to perhaps 10 percent of its center frequency. Thus a 1 GHz narrowband source might generate output energy over a bandwidth of from 20 or 30 up to perhaps 100 MHz. A wideband source uses either a very narrow pulse (bandwith is inversely proportional to pulse width) or a mechanism like a spark gap that is, in effect, a noise generator and inherently generates energy over a broad frequency range. If the target parameters are well enough known that an optimum frequency for coupling and energy deposition can be estimated, a narrowband source is likely to be optimum, especially if the center frequency can be tuned. Wideband sources offer the possibility of getting at least some energy into the target regardless of its details.
- Number of pulses: As mentioned earlier, sources can be single shot or rep rated. The former will generally have the greatest instantaneous output power, while the latter can hit the target with multiple pulses and thus have higher probability of radiating a pulse at the optimum angle to couple into the target. This, in turn, may reduce the required power level per shot to achieve a given probability of effect and thus increase the effective range of the weapon.
- Frequency range: Most practical sources operate somewhere between 200 MHz and 2 GHz. We have emphasized the number and complexity of frequency-dependent phenomena involved in an HPRF/HPM engagement, and the choice of an optimum frequency is far from simple. Higher frequencies mean smaller antenna sizes for a given gain, but lower frequencies tend to couple better to the POE structures found in many targets.

- Pulse length: For most sources, there is a trade-off between output power and pulse duration. As a rule of thumb, Level 1 and 2 effects tend to be triggered by crossing a certain instantaneous power threshold and thus favor a source trade-off toward high peak power at shorter pulse widths, while Level 3 requires deposition of enough energy to cause thermal damage in components and may require longer pulse lengths. The details depend heavily on the characteristics of a given source.
- Efficiency: The higher the source efficiency, the smaller and lighter the power system that drives it can be. Since efficiency varies widely by source type, this may be a primary consideration in optimizing an overall EM weapon. A source with low efficiency may lead to an impractical system weight once the prime and pulse power elements are accounted for.

While it is impractical here to give even a partial catalog of candidate sources, figure 5–3 lists a few specific examples to indicate the range of alternatives. Only tube sources are given, all of which can be considered more or less narrowband, since these are the leading candidates to achieve munitions-class performance in a reasonable time frame. Even advanced solid state power source concepts using advanced materials like silicon carbide and gallium nitride promise device powers only in the kilowatt region and thus would have to be used in phased arrays combining large numbers of individual transmitters to achieve the necessary performance. The examples are chosen from Barker and Schamiloglu.[8]

Figure 5–3. **Frequency in the Use of Attack Weapons in Terrorist Attacks Source**

Tube Type	Peak Output Power	Pulse Length	Pulse Repetition Rate	Efficiency	Approximate Weight
Magnetically Isolated Line Oscillator (MILO)	2 GW	140 nS	Single Shot	10%	Tube - 100 kg Total System -- 600-1200 kg
Relativistic Klystron Oscillator (RKO)	1.5 GW	120 nS	Single Shot	30%	Tube - 550 kg Total System -- 600-1000 kg
Reltron	0.6 GW	300 nS	50 Hz	40%	Tube - 60 kg
Relativistic Magnetron	3 GW	80 nS	Single Shot	10%	Tube ≥ 300 kg

We will take this as a representative threat and look next at how it might be used against friendly information systems to degrade the quality of theater C2.

Operational Implications of EM Attack

Typical C2 Information Processes

To have a context for assessing this threat, we will first postulate a simple model of C2 information processes, emphasizing the operational or theater level of war. However, to be meaningful the discussion must at least touch on tactical aspects such as the time line of the Find/Fix/Track/Target/Engage/Assess (F2T2EA) kill chain for time critical targets, because it may be in such circumstances that EM attack has its greatest effectiveness. This section builds on material originally presented at an HPM Technology Interchange Meeting on modeling and simulation of electronic attack.[9] The specific examples are airpower-centric, but parallels to C2 information processes in maritime and land components are easily drawn.

Figure 5–4 sketches a notional C2 structure intended to illustrate key information infrastructure and processes. While it does not literally represent an actual information architecture, it is typical of the kind of force internetting that has been demonstrated successfully in recent exercises. It includes:

- a variety of sensors communicating via one or more intelligence/surveillance/reconnaissance (ISR) networks
- an intelligence node (the Distributed Common Ground Station (DCGS) is pictured) where sensor feeds are fused and exploited
- a Battle Command Center where real-time battle management, replanning, and force tasking are carried out and communicated to both strike aircraft and ISR sensors
- precision-guided munitions, which employ both data links and GPS/INU guidance to hit within lethal range of target coordinates
- The strike aircraft tasked to prosecute a time-critical target.

Such a force depends heavily, sometimes critically, on a number of information processes, including the following:

- Planning: A computer-intensive process centered on production of a daily Air Tasking Order, Airspace Control Order, ISR Collection

Plan, and additional documents dealing with logistics, airlift, and other aspects of running the air war.

- Communications: The ability to exchange large volumes of data rapidly, using a variety of data links and other communications channels, despite hostile actions and the effects of the natural environment (e.g., disruptions caused by peaks in solar activity, such as sun spots).
- Situational assessment and awareness: The ability to import, fuse, analyze, and share information in ways that provide decision makers with the basis for sound tactical assessments and effective force management decisions.
- Human-machine interactions and collaboration services: The ability to visualize information, share relevant information across communities of interest, and accept human commands in ways that facilitate understanding, support timely decisions, and reduce individual workloads.
- Decision aiding and battle management: Closely allied to planning and situational assessment, but focused on real-time-development and assessment of alternatives, providing alerts for urgent situations and automating the formulation and execution of operational directions.
- Position, navigation, and timing (PNT): Services derived from GPS and other sources that enable force elements to position themselves, perform absolute and relative navigation, synchronize operations, deliver precision munitions based on target coordinates, and perform route planning to avoid threats and terrain obstacles.
- Data archiving and retrieval: The ability to store large volumes of data about the battlespace, friendly and hostile forces, terrain, weather, and other content relevant to operations and to access and present that data in real or near-real time to meet the needs of decision makers and war fighters.
- Platform control: The ability to plan, re-plan, and control the operations of UAVs, satellites, and manned platforms in response to the operational situation and current needs.

Every one of these processes is potentially susceptible to EM attack. If we set aside for the present discussion cyber attacks, such as injecting false data or malicious computer code and using sophisticated spoofing methods to issue false commands to platforms and systems, the primary threats come down to two: jamming of sensors and communications and disruption or damage of computers and networks. We must now consider the feasibility and consequences of these attacks.

Figure 5–4. **Elements of an Internetted Joint Force Tasked to Locate and Strike Time-Critical Targets**

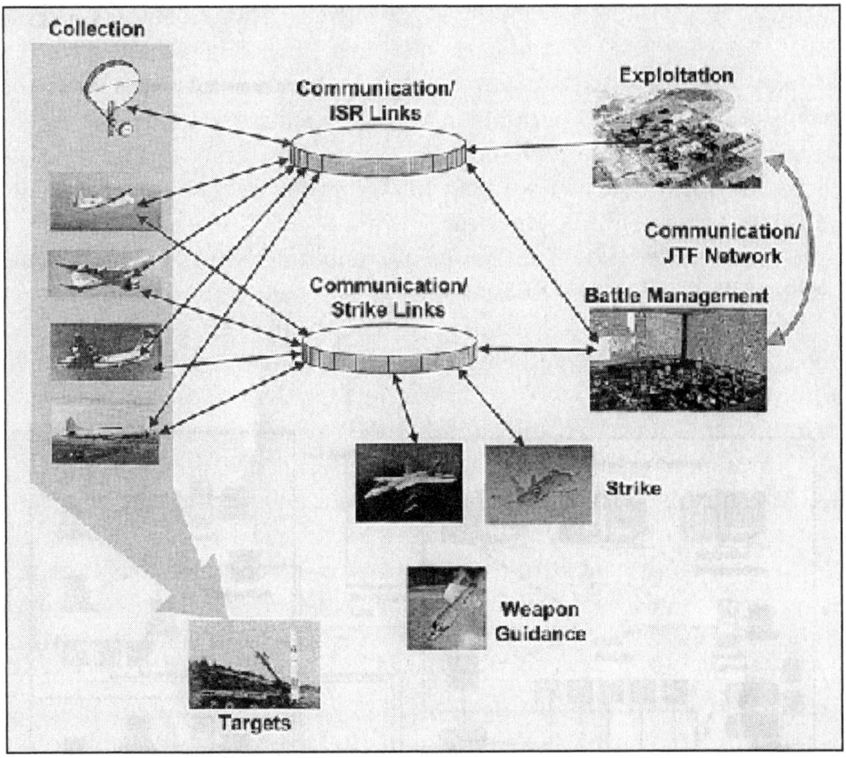

EM Attack on Sensors

Low Power EM Attack

Methods for jamming or deceiving sensors, traditionally called electronic countermeasures (ECM), are well known, as are a variety of techniques for defeating them, called electronic counter-countermeasures (ECCM). Effective ECM can be an important mode of EM attack, especially in tactical situations where delay in detection of the location or activities of a hostile entity allows it to either accomplish its mission or escape an attack by friendly forces. For example, if a hostile mobile missile battery is protected by a jammer that masks it from detection by friendly surveillance radar for the few minutes required to fire and move to a protected location, it achieves a significant tactical success.

At the operational level, ECM is less of an issue because the objective of friendly ISR forces is to build up an overall picture of the battle space, including a time history of hostile movements and communications. Jamming tends to be only locally effective, and advanced sensors include ever more capable ECCM to deal with older ECM systems and methods. Moreover, as our ability to put multiple, complementary sensors in the battle space increases, the ability to jam a particular radar or other sensor becomes less effective. Even the mobile missile battery may find itself attacked if its movements have been tracked in the intervals when friendly ISR systems could not be jammed.

A good example of the power of combining sensor methods is the ability of the E-8 Joint STARS platform to alternate ground moving target indication (GMTI) and synthetic aperture radar (SAR) imaging modes such that a hostile unit on the move is detected and tracked by the former, while the latter can be invoked if the unit stops. During Operation *Desert Storm*, some E-8 crews became fond of the slogan, "If you move, you die, and if you stop, you die." As multiple sensors, using diverse sensing modalities on a mixture of manned platforms, UAVs, and satellites are emplaced and their outputs fused in near-real time, it will become increasingly difficult for an opponent to use EM weapons successfully. This becomes even truer when these sensors can stare persistently and over large areas to build up patterns of hostile activity over time and, when this data is analyzed, to predict the significance of hostile activity and future moves (referred to as Predictive Battle Space Awareness). In short, an opponent with sufficiently capable ECM systems may be able to defeat friendly forces in individual encounters, but will find it increasingly difficult at the operational level to deny friendly C2 processes the knowledge they need to plan and execute decisive operations.

HPRF/HPM Attack

If the opponent possesses EM weapons capable of inducing Level 2 or 3 effects, the situation becomes potentially more serious. By disabling key nodes in a sensor network for significant periods of time, the enemy could blind friendly forces sufficiently to allow force movements and attacks that achieve surprise and success. However, as noted earlier, these EM attacks are inherently limited in range and require radiated energy to be pointed onto the target. They are therefore likely to be most effective against fixed targets such as ground radar sites, rather than mobile sensor platforms such as manned or unmanned aircraft. By housing ground sensors in well-constructed metal vans or shelters and providing protection against coupling of damaging electrical transients through available POEs, friendly forces can harden sensors significantly against electronic attack, requiring EM energy to be delivered at very close range. An attacker then might find that a conventional warhead is as effective as an EM weapon and a great deal less expensive. Low and high power EM attacks on sensors cannot be ignored, but good system design and reasonable measures to protect high value assets can mitigate the risk. This is not the major threat posed by these weapons.

EM Attack on Communications

Communications can be attacked by EM weapons, either by disrupting information nodes or by jamming or damaging the channels themselves. The first of these is a variant on computer network attack and will be considered in the next subsection. Here, we will evaluate direct attacks on communications channels. Level 1 effects are the most likely and will be considered in the following paragraphs.

In the emerging concepts and architecture of the DOD Transformational Communications System (TCS), broadband terrestrial links, especially fiber optics, will be used to the maximum extent possible to connect fixed sites. DOD has committed to heavy investment in terrestrial optical fiber channels in support of this objective, which promises to deliver very high capacity, highly secure communications between the continental United States (CONUS) and operational theaters, terminating in teleports or points of presence in or adjacent to any given AO. Such communications are largely immune to EM attack in any form other than the damage or disruption of electronics in the nodes that access the fiber channels. Similar terrestrial channels among nodes within a theater of operations have the same relative vulnerability.

The primary concern, therefore, centers on the links between and among fixed nodes and platforms or units on the move. Various communications media, such as the Army Tactical Warfighter Internet, using systems like the Enhanced Position Location Reporting system, the Link 16 standard tactical data link (TDL), and the Navy Cooperative Engagement Capability system, can be jammed and can resist jamming by their waveform design and modes of operation. The same is true of the emerging family of ISR networks based on the Common Data Link (CDL) and including the Tactical CDL (TCDL) and the Multi Platform CDL (MP-CDL). These systems employ various combinations of directional antennas, satellite relays, coding, and spread spectrum techniques to improve their ability to function in the face of jamming. They also benefit from the inherent mobility of their users—a jammer typically must track a specific node and subject it to jamming in order to cause more than a fleeting interruption of communications.

The operational impact of such jamming is highly time and situation dependent. A jammer that causes a message sequence to be dropped at a critical point in an engagement may be very effective, while one that simply delays by a few milliseconds the delivery of routine traffic may not. Communications protocols that implement "reliable" messaging, i.e., that can detect communication failures and compensate by retransmission or use of alternative channels, can largely negate such jamming and should be an essential design feature of communications systems involved in combat operations. Responsibility for detecting lost messages and taking action to recover from them is a fundamental design consideration for C2 software developers, while finer-grained error detection and correction can be built into networks. In short, EM attacks on communications can have significant operational impact, including the communications equivalent of a "lucky shot," but only if friendly systems lack the ability to detect and correct for errors and outages due to hostile actions. As a practical matter, persistent failures of interoperability among the "stovepiped" communications systems developed by the various Services are likely to have greater negative operational impact than jamming by an opponent.

EM Attack on Computer Networks

A much thornier problem is presented by EM weapons that can produce effects at Levels 1, 2, or 3 on the computer systems and networks that enable modern command and control (C2) processes. A typical C2 node may include hundreds of computers, both workstations and servers, connected by a hierarchy of LANs, and depending heavily on data bases, planning and collaboration tools, and communication channels to command and control for a range of military and civilian operations. Moreover, the electronics that equip these centers are likely to consist largely of commercial products, perhaps with some "ruggedization," and to be housed in local facilities ranging from tents to rented office buildings. Given an opponent or threat agent who can muster EM weapons of the sort described earlier in this chapter, there may be grounds for concern about susceptibility to EM attack.

As a start on assessing this threat, we begin with the very simple C2 network operations node composed of three basic cells sketched in figure 5–5. The figure shows an operations center where business functions such as air traffic control, telecommunications operations, and military operations are monitored and directed in real time, a strategic operations function where the initial plans for enterprise-support operations are developed, and a network monitoring-and-control function where information sensor and other equipment feeds are collected and assessed. The node is connected by an overall LAN that is protected by encryption, and each functional cell has a local LAN and file server (secure communications devices are shown in red).

Figure 5–5. **Notional Command and Control Node**

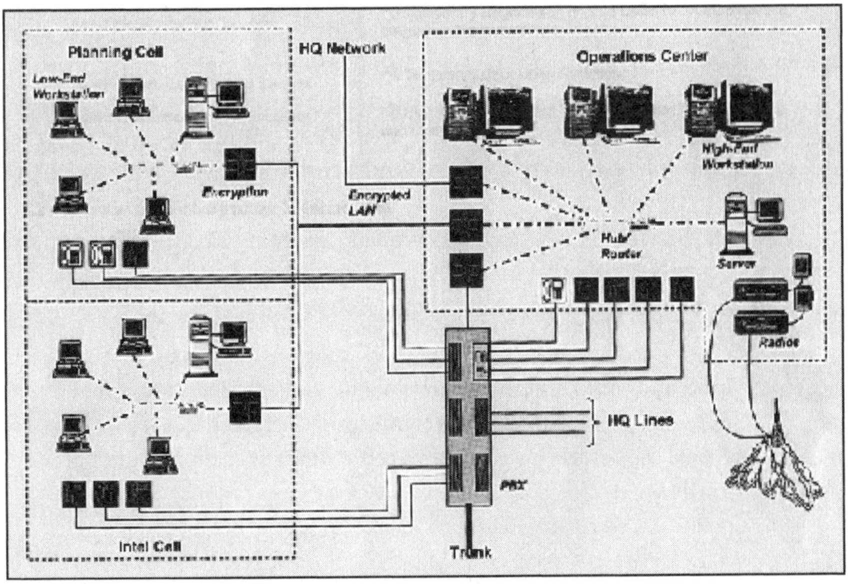

The operations center is on a separate network connected to the enterprise's headquarters, and the node has both telecommunications links and backup radios. We assume that this node is tracking and managing current operations based on an initial operational plan with adjustments being made as the situation requires. It is also likely monitoring information sensor and other equipment inputs and feeding them to control and strategic planning staffs, and is assessing the developing plans for the next operational time period.

To assess how an EM attack would impact such a node, we will postulate a sequence of activities and consider the consequences of various disruptions. Susceptibilities to EM attack include:

- disabling of individual workstations, resulting in the inability of the associated function or operator to deliver a required output such as a plan, situational assessment, or operational tasking
- loss of network message traffic, resulting in failure or delay of C2 node functions including maintaining a current operation, developing and assessing alternative courses of action, and issuing appropriate tasking to network operators
- denial of access to stored information files or corruption of file contents, resulting in erroneous analysis and ineffective orders to operators.

Denial of external communications can result from inaccurate operational assessment, failure to identify and respond to threats or opportunities, and inaccurate communications regarding enterprise and operational information. One plausible scenario involves the detection of a time-critical target, like a quickly evolving and regenerating network worm or virus attack, the tasking of an operational unit to attack the target, confirmation that the tasking has been received and is being executed, and analysis of the damage assessment of the results. A basic sequence of events, absent hostile interference, might be the following:

- network monitoring-and-control cell receives information sensor inputs and confirms the existence of an attack and identifies activities to install software patches to mitigate the target attack
- network monitoring-and-control cell notifies operations center of the attack
- operations center evaluates available mission-critical network resources, selects a tactical approach to minimize and correct the attack, and formulates and sends a tasking message
- tasked network control center receives the message, acknowledges the tasking, and initiates the corrections
- network monitoring-and-control cell executes the tactical approach and provides immediate assessment of its success
- operations center tasks the network monitoring-and-control cell to perform verification that corrective actions are in place

- network monitoring-and-control cell collects and analyzes information sensor output, and sends it to the operations center.

Now we assume that the opponent delivers an EM weapon against the C2 node as critical network functions, transfer of sensitive information, or information upgrade are being performed. We assume first that the weapon induces Level 1 effects, which randomly interrupt several of the steps in the above sequence for anywhere from less than a minute to a small number of minutes, but do not fundamentally disrupt the synchronization of activities within the node. We further assume that the network operations require several minutes for each stage of the network functions to be performed. In this case, the degradation of the timeline of the network node is such that it can still execute the sequence of steps required to successfully complete its operations.

However, if the Level 1 effects are pervasive, such that many operators within the C2 node lose the continuity of their own activities (e.g., screens go blank or important network messages are dropped) and coordination among related activities is broken, the overall decision process may be so disrupted that extensive communication among operators and information retrieval is needed to get the node back into harmonious operation. This might well delay the download or transfer of critical operational information, especially in high performance safety operations such as air traffic control or nuclear or power system control, and the disruption would be especially severe if involved staffs were surprised by the event and inadequately trained to recognize and recover from it. Even if the attack were successful, an EM weapon that delayed or defeated the corrective follow-up might cause unproductive, repeated commitment of resources to a threat that has not been confirmed as neutralized.

If the EM attack is able to cause Level 2 events, involving minutes to an hour or more to restore effective C2 functions, the time-critical target is quite likely to execute its mission (i.e., install a Trojan horse, time bomb, access root) and survive. If Level 3 effects occur, disabling one or more key C2 node functions for perhaps several hours, strategic and operational management would be degraded to such an extent that operations probably would degenerate to uncoordinated actions of individual units. Presumably these units would be well trained and would make the best of the tactical situation, using their own information sources and inputs directly from locally available information sensors, backup C2 nodes, and preplanned contingency plans and procedural methods. Even so, the result could easily be a major, even decisive, advantage for an opponent poised to exploit the disorganization such an event triggers.

This kind of time critical scenario is something of a worst case. In other circumstances, if an opponent delivered an EM weapon that disrupted or damaged C2 functions, perhaps delaying a planning cycle or forcing the enterprise to shift to a backup center, or even completely disrupt operations, the effect would be equivalent to delivering a successful conventional strike or carrying out physical sabotage. The increasingly information-centric nature of our military and commercial operations makes it clear that disruption of the underlying information processes will diminish our ability to carry out tasks and may create very worrisome opportunities for an opponent who cannot match our technology but can interfere with its operation.

Protecting Against EM Attack

The EM attacks we have been considering involve upset, disruption, or damage to friendly C2 information systems as a result of either jamming or deception, or of delivery of electrical transients to sensitive electronics. The first of these can be dealt with by a combination of robust ECCM and, more important, deployment of sensor and communication systems that are distributed, use diverse modalities and pathways, and explicitly provide for the detection of hostile interference and for recovery from its effects.

Protection against HPRF/HPM weapons comes down to careful design to prevent damaging transients from being delivered to sensitive components or, if they do arrive, from causing system crashes or erroneous computations. Among these design considerations are the following:

- Lightning protection, e.g., placing surge arrestors on external cabling, can provide a measure of resistance to EM attack. However, the energy in a lightning transient (as well as an EMP event) is concentrated at relatively low frequencies, typically well below 100 MHz. Therefore, these devices may not be as effective in blocking EM weapon energy at 200 MHz to 2 GHz.
- Bonded enclosures or Faraday cages, which are basically metal chambers with good electrical connectivity across their seams and features such as wire screens across windows and other openings, can effectively prevent radiated EM energy from entering a system, especially if they have solid earth grounds. This suggests that C2 nodes be deployed and housed in suitable shelters.

- Cable and antenna protection, which can take the form of connectors that include ferrite beads around individual conductors and various other kinds of transient limitation, can minimize the ability of an EM weapon to use these penetrations of a shielded enclosure as ports of entry.
- Power supply filtering or extending commercial lightning protection to the higher frequencies will reduce the possibility that damaging transients will be coupled in via the power lines.
- Fault tolerant data storage, such as the Redundant Array of Independent Disks (RAID) approach to disk storage, reduces the chances that failure or contamination of one disk drive will cause data loss.
- Robust network cabling to include fiber optics and twisted-pair differential conductors that are less susceptible to acting as antennas on which EM energy can induce damaging transient voltages, plus surge protection devices at network terminations.
- Reliable network messaging protocols that have features to detect and compensate for failed delivery of messages or packets.
- Robust software applications that are designed to tolerate dropped messages, erroneous data values, and other induced errors by "riding through" such events.

An additional protective measure is to subject C2 systems to controlled testing in which they are subjected to simulated EM weapon transients and instrumented to determine how they respond. This may support product choices, design of equipment enclosures, selection of networks, and other features so as to minimize susceptibility to EM attack. It can also quantify the vulnerability of systems and thus allow assessment of the threat posed by EM weapons known or postulated to be in hostile hands.

Conclusions and Recommendations

The Reality of the EM Threat

The threat to friendly C2 systems and processes from EM weapons that can be assembled from available technologies and products is real. High power radio frequency and microwave sources are used in commercial applications ranging from communications to the accelerated drying of green lumber. Even relatively crude EM weapons that can be mounted in innocuous delivery platforms like commercial vehicles may be brought to bear, especially against deployed C2 facilities, and have the potential to cause disruption if not damage. Continuing progress in HPRF/HPM technology for both military and commercial applications will steadily increase the EM weapon capabilities available to our enemies.

If we ignore this threat, we make ourselves vulnerable to it. Friendly systems that use unhardened commercial components and are installed, due to logistic or political constraints, in unshielded facilities may be especially susceptible to EM attacks. EM attacks against sensors and communications may produce local and temporary operational effects and may, on occasion, lead to tactical successes by an opponent, but are less significant at the operational level of war than disturbances in the C2 nodes that maintain operational pictures for commanders and exercise control of forces.

On the other hand, straightforward design methods exist to mitigate this threat. The preferred approach is a layered defense in which each element of an integrated information system is designed for maximum hardness against EM effects without unduly compromising performance or cost. If the only available housing for a C2 node is a tent or a clapboard hut, then the electronics can be mounted in bonded cases to provide effective shielding and interconnected with transient-resistant networks. EM weapon effects and susceptibilities can be determined in controlled testing, typically using both anechoic chambers for complete control of the EM environment and field testing to simulate real world conditions.

The physical phenomena involved in EM attack are complex and hard to predict, but they are not black magic. Systems that are thoughtfully designed from the outset to account for these threats and to both minimize the possibility of disruption and tolerate momentary disturbances can neutralize the EM weapons likely to be encountered for some time to come.

EM weapons represent a relatively new threat whose significance derives mainly from the fact that we have massively committed our military doctrine and tactics to information-enabled operations. Essentially, the concern is that information processes of enormous power may be defeated by disruptive techniques available to enemies who come nowhere near to matching our level of technology, and that the result will be to deprive us of the operational advantage we seek from Information Dominance. The greatest danger is that we will ignore this threat and fail to protect our systems. The threat is real, but the means to mitigate it are also real. The imperative is to track the evolving EM weapon threat and to discipline our system development and operational processes in ways that ensure that it does not imperil our success.

A Prudent Course of Action

Many of the recommendations supported by the argument of this paper also have been suggested in other chapters of this book. Specifically:

- The status of and trends in EM weaponry in the hands of nations and organizations hostile to U.S. interests should continue to be a matter of priority in intelligence collection and analysis.
- Sensor and communications systems that allow multidimensional measurement of the battle space, protect against interference, and provide diverse, robust, high-capacity connectivity for information exchange should be deployed so as to defeat hostile attempts to prevent the collection and distribution of information.
- Command and control systems should be designed with a comprehensive strategy to protect against EM attack, from the enclosures in which they are housed to the utilities that support their operation to the hardware and software components that implement their information processes.

Notes

The author is deeply grateful to colleagues in the Air Force Research Laboratory, Directed Energy Directorate, and in the firms that support its HPRF/HPM programs for their contributions to the assessment presented in this paper. Dr. Robert L. Hutchins of Northrop Grumman Corporation performed much of the analysis summarized here, reviewed the manuscript of this paper, and provided many helpful suggestions.

[1] Office of the Chairman, Joint Chiefs of Staff, *Joint Vision 2020* (Washington, D.C.: DOD, 2001).

[2] A typical example is *DOD Information Security: Serious Weaknesses Continue to Place Defense Operations at Risk*, Report to the Secretary of Defense, General Accounting Office Report GAO/AIMD-99-107 (Washington, D.C.: GAO, August 1999).

[3] The terms *susceptibility* and *vulnerability* are often used interchangeably. Strictly speaking, susceptibility refers to the "hardness" of a system to EM attack (i.e., the maximum level of energy that can be injected into the system by an EM weapon before upset, disruption, or damage will occur), whereas vulnerability is defined from the viewpoint of the weapon as the minimum level of injected energy required to ensure that EM effects are induced.

[4] See, for example, David A. Fulghum, "USAF Acknowledges Beam Weapon Readiness," *Aviation Week & Space Technology*, October 7, 2002, 27–28.

[5] Clayborne D. Taylor and D. V. Giri, *High Power Microwave Systems and Effects* (Washington, D.C.: Taylor and Francis, 1994); K. S. H. Lee (ed.), *EMP Interaction: Principles, Techniques, and Reference Data* (Washington, D.C.: Taylor and Francis, 1986); Tesche, Ianoz, and Karlsson, *EMC Analysis Methods and Computational Models* (New York: Wiley, 1996).

[6] The decibel, abbreviated dB, is a logarithmic scale for expressing the ratio of two power levels. Each 10 dB means an additional factor of 10. Thus, 10 dB of attenuation by a wall means that the power after passing through the wall is one tenth what it was arriving at the wall, and an antenna gain of 60 dB means that the amplitude of the radiated beam is 1,000,000 times stronger than if the power were radiated equally in all directions.

[7] C. E. Baum, "Maximization of Electromagnetic Response at a Distance," *IEEE Transactions on EMC* 34(3): 148–53 (August 1992).

[8] Barker and Schamiloglu, *High Power Microwave Sources and Technologies* (New York: IEEE Press, (2001).

[9] Hutchins, Villamarin, and Borky, "Role of Network and Fault Tree Models for Determining HPM Lethality of Electronic Systems," (paper presented at the HPM ELMS Technology Interchange Meeting, Air Force Research Laboratory, Kirtland AFB, NM, (2001) March 19–20, 2002).

Chapter 6

Vulnerabilities to Electromagnetic Attack of the Civil Infrastructure

Donald C. Latham

The inexorable and deepening dependency on information in the modern business world has led to greatly increased complexity in the technical infrastructure that collects, manipulates, and delivers a plethora of information products and services. This complexity, in turn, is leading to an increased set of potential vulnerabilities, which the civil sector is largely unaware of or has chosen to ignore. The average American has little awareness that moving U.S. troops, as well as their equipment and supplies, to overseas locations increasingly depends on facilities that are a critical part of the civil infrastructure. Even the temporary disruption or shutdown by electromagnetic (EM) attack on a power facility, port, or railroad could be quite serious to the projection of forces abroad, especially if the movement is time critical.

The civil emphasis of attention to electronic-related vulnerabilities has focused largely on so-called cyber warfare, involving rogue hackers attacking computer systems or injecting damaging software viruses through the Internet or other local and global networks. Yet physical attack and insider sabotage are also quite possible. In fact, insider sabotage is a serious problem and must be addressed by more thorough and intrusive vetting of employees with critical access to telecommunications, networks, computers, servers, and other related equipment and software.

Although these vulnerabilities are real and must be addressed, added to them is the not-so-well-known or -understood susceptibility of the civil infrastructure to attack by EM devices, which are, by their nature, silent and stealthy weapons. This chapter describes one potential form of electronic warfare (EW) attack on a civil facility such as a major banking data and communications center, a commercial communications satellite terminal facility, an electric power switching center, or perhaps even a Federal Aviation Administration (FAA) regional air traffic control center. Effects from an EW attack on facilities such as these could range from a minor disruption of operations to severe damage that shuts down the operation for hours or days. Table 1 lists some examples of critical civil infrastructure and the associated potential vulnerabilities and consequences if subjected to EM attack.

Table – 1:
Potential Civil Infrastructure Vulnerabilities

Example – Critical Information Related Infrastructure	**Example – Potential Vulnerabilities to Information Attack**
Commercial Communications Satellite Systems	✍ EM Attack of Terrestrial SATCOM Control Facilities ✍ UpLink Intrusion of TT&C Links
Terrestrial Cellular Communications Systems	✍ Jamming Cellular Control and Transmission Facilities
Computer Data Centers	✍ High Power Electromagnetic Energy Attack to Induce Computer Upset & Burnout
Federal and Commercial Banking Facilities	✍ Cripple the Banking Computer & Communications Systems in Largely Unprotected Facilities
FAA Air Traffic Control Centers	✍ Temporary Degradation or Shut Down of FAA Computers, Displays, Communications
Wired-Telephone Switching Centers	✍ Temporary Shut Down Switches
Power Generation Control Facilities	✍ High Power EM Attack Temporarily Shut Down Switching and Control Systems

Attacks such as those in table 1 could be carried out by a powerful EM system. To make an attack possible, the equipment would be placed close to the target facility and would then unleash a burst of EM radiation directed by an antenna. Some of the impinging radiation likely would couple into the facility. If it does so with sufficient power, the results, as described in chapter 4, could range from a brief upset to immediate serious physical damage to electronic systems. The effects depend on many complex factors such as the building construction and any EM protective measures that were taken during design and construction. In fact, the effects perceived by personnel in the facility or picked up on remote monitors may resemble a "standard" crash of a computer or server or the effects of a lightning strike. In other words, the people operating the facility quite possibly will not know they have been attacked by an EW weapon.

The most likely scenario is that an EM attack is one component or tier of an attack on a major civil infrastructure that may also involve chemical, biological, or explosive weapons. The EW attack may be used to add to the confusion and could be used to slow down or degrade the responses to a more devastating component of a multitiered attack. For example, denying communications, even for a while, to first responders such as firemen and police could be a significant factor in how a city responds to an assault and how many lives can be saved.

The fundamentals of EM attack systems and the EM attack problem, effects, and mechanisms are described in chapter 5 of this book and in other chapters. These fundamentals will be used as the basis for framing the challenges to deterring and defeating potential EM attacks on critical civil infrastructure.

Protecting the Civil Infrastructure Against EM Attack

Perhaps the most challenging task in addressing critical civil infrastructure protection against EM attacks is the general lack of awareness of the potential threat and its consequences by the civilian population—especially by the executives who build and manage these critical facilities. For example, major U.S. banking industries rely on a network of high-speed communications links between banks and large telecommunications switching centers. These switching centers are numerous and are located across the 50 states to provide highly reliable communications (typically at T–1 rates of 1.45 MB/s) for funds transfers and customer account transactions. Physically locating these facilities is relatively easy using Web-based data on the Internet. In general, with the exception of lightning guards, the buildings housing these centers are not designed with EM protection systems. The EM frequency spectrum of lightning tends to be about 10 MHz and lower. Thus, lightning protection would not shield a building from the effects of an EM weapon operating at much higher frequencies.

Because many of the critical civil infrastructure capabilities are vital to the Department of Defense (DOD) for protecting U.S. forces overseas, DOD is conducting analyses of these facilities and examining how to mitigate any disruption in their capabilities and operations. The unresolved issue is who is to fund the "fixes" to identified vulnerabilities. The issues of ownership, dual use, and dual payoff to mitigate the vulnerability to both the civil owner and the U.S. government are complicated. Technically, the means are available to design and construct well-protected facilities against EM attacks even to Level 3 if necessary. Retrofitting protection into existing facilities can be done, but at higher costs and disruption.

A prioritized approach to civil infrastructure protection needs to be developed. The new Federal Department of Homeland Security (DHS) has primary responsibility for this task along with DOD involvement and support. The government must include the civil industries considered critical to U.S. national security and economic security to participate with DOD and DHS in resolving issues related to vulnerability assessment and funding.

Financial models exist that address the challenges involved with who pays and how. For example, from the 1960s to 1980s, the U.S. government authorized AT&T to add a small "tax" to their long-line rates to pay for improving the survival of certain DOD nuclear command, control, and communications lines and associated facilities. The upgraded, more survivable facilities included underground and "hardened" switching centers, which were also protected against nuclear weapon generated electromagnetic pulse effects.

In this era of increased concern about terrorism and homeland security in a national security context, it might be feasible to create a "Homeland Security Tax" (HST) akin to Medicare, to which all taxpayers contribute at a fixed, small percentage (1.45 percent, again like Medicare) of their income. This HST would be a fenced account to be allocated back to local, county, and State Homeland Security initiatives. These initiatives could include partial compensation to improve the survival of critical civil infrastructure such as communication systems, chemical warfare and biological warfare sensor systems, and some level of protection against EM attacks on critical electronic systems.

An Electromagnetic Terrorist Attack Scenario

Let us suppose that some terrorist group has decided on a multi-pronged attack of a major U.S. facility or set of facilities. The terrorists plan to release a combination of explosive weapons against various subway stations as well as a biological agent in several locations of a major subway and to conduct an EM attack to shut down the subway temporarily, thereby trapping several thousand people in below-ground tunnels and stations.

All of the equipment needed to launch this type of an attack is available commercially, off the shelf. (A detailed description of equipment and methodology to launch the attack was provided as part of the workshop discussion.)

The primary subway control facilities are easily located, typically in above-ground facilities, and very likely are not designed to cope with any EM effects worse than ordinary lightning. Typical lightning protection devices are not effective in stopping much higher frequency EM energy devices (weapons) such as the EM system in the possession of our hypothetical terrorist group. Chapter 5 discusses the end-to-end analysis of how to attack a facility containing the type of electronic equipment to be found in a modern subway control center or a local police command center. (A blended attack such as multiple EM attacks or an EM and physical attack launched simultaneously would naturally be even more difficult to recover from.) A major problem with any form of EM attack is for the attacker to assess rapidly (near real-time, if possible) the level of success of his attack. Thus, "bomb damage assessment" after an EM attack is both difficult to accomplish and uncertain in its accuracy. For example, a high-power EM attack against a system may have succeeded by crippling the data processors and associated communication equipment, even though the networked sensors appear to be operating normally right after the attack. Determining what has happened inside the system is not easy, maybe even impossible, and thus, the risk for the attacker is whether to prolong the assault or quickly make assumptions about the results.

Findings and Conclusions

Conceivably, EM attacks against the civil infrastructure could be carried out using readily available commercial components, and thus, the threat is real. The dollar cost and technical complexity to design and build an EM weapon as described in this chapter is relatively low risk and manageable.

So far, civil sector facilities such as communication centers, satellite ground control centers, industrial control facilities, banking telecommunications centers, and many others appear to have not considered EM attacks in their design. These unshielded facilities may be especially vulnerable, and thus, real disruption of related operations could occur. An EM attack would quite likely be used along with explosive, chemical, or biological attacks to create confusion, delay responses, and create more panic.

Well-understood technologies are available to design in protection of entire buildings or rooms within buildings against EM attack. Because retrofitting protection can be much more difficult and expensive, this EM hardening should be designed into the building and to the electronics it is going to house from the beginning. Either way, the solution is not easily found or put into effect. But the difficulty should not deter us; the threat cannot be ignored. This EM threat is yet another new challenge with which the law enforcement and intelligence communities will have to deal. The already huge and growing dependence on information systems in our economy and everyday lives makes this issue a significant concern and warrants ongoing analysis.

Chapter 7

Trends in Cyber Vulnerabilities, Threats, and Countermeasures

Michael A. Vatis

The terrorist attacks of September 11, 2001, taught the United States a painful lesson: The fact that existing or potential adversaries have not previously deployed a certain method of attack does not mean they will not use the method in the future. Terrorists have shown a willingness to embrace new and unconventional methods of war that rely, to some extent, on the element of surprise, and we can expect they will continue to do so. If we do not prepare to defend against novel modes of attack, then we will remain vulnerable to potentially catastrophic attacks of all kinds. The rapid and quickening pace of technological change makes it even more urgent not only that we anticipate what future methods of attack might be but also that we take active measures to understand and prepare for those methods as soon as they become reasonably foreseeable, not after they are used against us. Given the increasing availability of destructive technologies to both state and nonstate actors with considerable malice against the United States, "fighting the last war" is simply not an option. We must prepare today to fight the wars of tomorrow.

To military thinkers and planners, the idea of preparing to fight tomorrow's wars rather than those of yesterday is a truism. Yet, remarkably, as a nation, we are falling into the trap of paying insufficient attention to a new threat to our national security—the threat of cyber attacks. In the cyber arena, the situation is, in some ways, worse than simply paying too little heed to a potential new threat until it manifests itself. Threats in the cyber arena have manifested themselves. We are reminded constantly of our vulnerabilities to the threat, yet we still are not doing enough. Every hour of every day, some individual or group is writing or disseminating a new disruptive virus or worm or is breaking into a computer network in the United States—probably even a Government-owned computer network—and stealing information or money, defacing a Web site, mapping a network for future attack, testing defenses, or planting a Trojan horse or digital time bomb for future use.[1] And yet, because we have not suffered a significant destructive cyber attack at the hands of a hostile nation-state or terrorist group, we continue to underestimate the potential harm that an attack of this kind could cause.

If this cyber threat were limited to economic harm that could be considered part of the "cost of doing business" by private companies, then we might take a different perspective. But it is not. Cyber attacks also pose a threat to national security. From this day forward, every significant military conflict involving the United States will likely include some aspect of information warfare—offensive, defensive, or both. The Department of Defense (DOD) has shown increased willingness to use offensive information warfare, at least for tactical purposes such as disabling an adversary's command, control, and communications networks or disrupting antiaircraft systems. Moreover, once policy with respect to broader uses of information warfare is established according to National Security Presidential Directive 16, DOD may extend its use of cyber attacks against broader targets such as an adversary's critical infrastructures.[2] At the same time, the United States will be the target of cyber attacks by adversaries seeking to strike a perceived Achilles heel of the United States—the dependence on information technology not only for communication but also for the operation of critical Government and civilian infrastructures as well as for military command and control. Because no nation can match the United States' conventional military or nuclear capabilities, this form of asymmetric attack will be a weapon of choice for future adversaries looking to level the playing field.

For years, cynics and skeptics have downplayed or ridiculed the notion of a cyber threat by saying either that the only real threat comes from American teenagers joyriding on networks or engaging in the cyber equivalent of vandalism or that the Government has over-hyped the problem to invent new missions in the post–Cold War world. But if kids can crash networks through "denial of service" or worm attacks or obtain system administrator level control of military or commercial networks, then surely it stands to reason that a sophisticated and well-funded foreign military or intelligence organization or a terrorist group could accomplish the same—and much worse. Indeed, the fact that our own Government has an offensive information warfare program should tell us something about the potential military utility of this form of assault.

Part of the difficulty in appreciating the full scope of the threat lies in the fact that the spectrum of potential malicious acts and the resulting effects are so broad. The wide range of attacks can include: politically motivated defacements or obstructions of Government and private company Web sites;[3] denial of service attacks against e-commerce, online news sites,[4] and Internet domain name root servers;[5] destructive worms and viruses affecting companies around the world;[6] intrusions by organized criminal groups into university and company networks for the sake of stealing proprietary information, credit card numbers, or money or to extort the system owner;[7] and intrusions into Government networks to steal sensitive information.[8] The sheer variety of potential attacks demonstrates not only that our information networks remain vulnerable but also that myriad bad actors are willing and able to exploit these vulnerabilities. Thus, the problem is not only a national security problem but also a counterintelligence problem, a law enforcement problem, and a business security problem. Because the vulnerability is, therefore, everybody's problem, the responsibility for fixing it remains unclear—at least at the level of defending against or preventing broadly destructive attacks with national effect. Moreover, the national security aspects of the threat—including information warfare, cyber-based espionage, and cyberterrorism—have been obscured amid the noise of other more visible and common forms of cyber attacks. This chapter therefore focuses on these aspects of the threat and on some of the challenges in dealing with them.

Information Warfare (a.k.a. Cyber Warfare or Computer Network Operations)

Information warfare is subject to varying definitions, but essentially involves the use of information systems to deny, exploit, corrupt, or destroy an adversary's information, information systems, and computer-based networks while protecting one's own. It, thus, has both offensive and defensive components. In this chapter, information warfare will refer specifically to nation-state use of computer-to-computer attacks and will not include other elements like propaganda or "psychological operations," which have been included in past DOD definitions of "information operations."[9]

At least several foreign nations have already developed information, or cyber, warfare doctrine, programs, and capabilities for use against each other, the United States, or other nations.[10] For example, in 1999, two Chinese military officers published a book promoting the use of unconventional measures, including the propagation of computer viruses, to counter the military power of the United States.[11]

Further complicating matters in the information warfare realm is the difficulty in distinguishing between state-sponsored information warfare and attacks by foreign civilians or groups who oppose U.S. Government policy or who have some other political motivation for attacking American computer networks. In early 2001, for instance, a loose coalition of Chinese hackers launched a widespread campaign of Web site defacements and "denial of service" attacks against Central Intelligence Agency (CIA) and White House Web sites. This coordinated attack was in direct response to the incident involving a collision between a U.S. surveillance plane and a Chinese fighter jet.[12] These attacks were not, as far as we know, specifically tied to the Chinese Government, but these types of attacks should cause us to consider the possibility of foreign nations covertly sponsoring attacks against the United States by seemingly unrelated groups or individuals.[13] Moreover, because disguising the origin of online attacks is relatively easy, the possibility exists that one nation (or a non-state actor) could launch a cyber attack against the United States while making it appear as though the attack were coming from another country (or non-state actor), thereby causing the United States to take retaliatory steps against the wrong entity.[14]

An episode known as "Solar Sunrise" illustrates the problems that might be caused by attribution of an attack to the wrong source. In February 1998, while the United States was sending troops and materiel to the Persian Gulf in anticipation of air strikes against Iraq, intruders broke into numerous DOD computers and obtained "root access"—meaning they had the same level of control of those networks as the system administrators and could have stolen or altered information or damaged the networks. The timing and nature of the intrusions led many in the Pentagon to believe initially that the Iraqi Government was behind the penetrations and that this incident was the first known instance of information warfare against the United States. These concerns were heightened when some of the intrusions were traced back to an Internet Service Provider (ISP) in the Persian Gulf region. Active countermeasures—both cyber and "kinetic"—were considered within the Pentagon, and President Clinton was briefed on the situation. However, a multiagency investigation led by the National Infrastructure Protection Center (NIPC) (which was just being established in those same weeks) in conjunction with Israeli and other foreign law enforcement agencies soon determined that the intrusions were, in fact, the work of two California teenagers, assisted by an Israeli teenager, and that the ISP in the Gulf region was merely one of many "hop sites" between the attack's point of origin in the United States and the victim networks.[15]

Espionage

Foreign intelligence services have been using cyber tools as part of their information gathering and espionage tradecraft since at least the 1980s. Between 1986 and 1989, in an incident immortalized in Clifford Stohl's book, *The Cuckoo's Egg*, a group of West German hackers penetrated numerous military, educational, and business networks in the United States, Europe, and Japan, stealing passwords, programs, and other information. They then sold this information to the Soviet Committee for State Security (KGB).[16] Although very little unclassified information exists with respect to current cyber espionage practices or trends, the limited information to which we do have access seems clearly to indicate that computer intrusions are a tool of choice for foreign intelligence services interested in acquiring sensitive U.S. Government and private sector information.[17]

Here, too, the problem of distinguishing between state-sponsored activity and that of autonomous actors is a difficult one. In the late 1990s, for example, the NIPC led an investigation, codenamed "Moonlight Maze," into a series of intrusions into numerous DOD, other Federal Government, and private sector networks. The intruder successfully accessed U.S. Government networks and took large amounts of unclassified but sensitive information, including defense technical research information. The investigation—which involved FBI field offices, DOD, and the intelligence community—ultimately traced the intrusions to Russia.[18] Although further details about the source of these attacks cannot be discussed publicly, it is evident that this method of collecting vast amounts of Government data has obvious attraction to foreign intelligence agencies.

Cyberterrorism

The term cyberterrorism is often used by the media and others to refer to any breach of computer security. This usage is highly misleading and not only causes confusion about the true nature and complexity of the cyber threat but also results in a loss of credibility on the part of the Government as it attempts to raise awareness about the broader issue of computer security. For this chapter, the term is used much more narrowly and refers to truly destructive computer-to-computer attacks that cause death, injury, significant economic loss, or significant disruption of a critical infrastructure and that are motivated by a desire to coerce or intimidate a government or civilian population in pursuit of some political, religious, or ideological end.[19]

Applying this definition, the United States has not yet experienced an instance of cyberterrorism. We can expect terrorists to continue to prefer kinetic attacks that cause large-scale death and destruction. Nevertheless, the relative ease, low cost, and low risk of engaging in computer-to-computer attacks—and the possibility of using them to impede Government response to a physical attack or to maximize the sense of public chaos attending a physical terrorism incident—make cyber attacks an attractive addition to terrorists' arsenals. In fact, ample indicators suggest that terrorists could begin using this weapon in the near future.

For starters, we have known for some time that terrorists use information technology and the Internet to formulate plans, raise funds, spread propaganda, and communicate securely.[20] For example, Ramzi Yousef, the mastermind of the 1993 World Trade Center bombing, stored detailed-plans to destroy U.S.-bound airliners in encrypted files on his laptop computer.[21] In addition, U.S. intelligence sources report that al Qaeda is using the Internet to reorganize forces that were scattered by the global war on terrorism and the downfall of the Taliban.[22] Terrorists, thus, are very familiar with the utility of information technology in their planning.

Moreover, at least one terrorist-affiliated group has already used relatively unsophisticated cyber attacks to disrupt its enemies' information systems. A group calling itself the Internet Black Tigers conducted a successful denial of service attack on servers of Sri Lankan Government embassies.[23] In addition, a Canadian Government report indicated that the Irish Republican Army considered the use of information operations against British interests.[24] Information about the cyber capabilities and intentions of al Qaeda is less than pellucid, but recent reports suggest that the cyber threat from this organization is real.[25] According to information found in seized computers or revealed by suspects during interrogations by U.S. or foreign officials, al Qaeda has been considering cyber attacks against U.S. infrastructure targets and has been researching cyber attack techniques.[26] It reportedly has also been gathering information about potential targets of cyber attacks, including the computer networks that control power, transportation, and communications.[27]

In April 2002, the CIA provided this assessment of the prospect of cyberterrorism to the Senate Select Committee on Intelligence:

> Cyberwarfare attacks against our critical infrastructure systems will become an increasingly viable option for terrorists as they become

> more familiar with these targets, and the technologies required to attack them. Various terrorist groups—including al-Qa'ida and Hizballah—are becoming more adept at using the Internet and computer technologies, and the FBI is monitoring an increasing number of cyber threats. . . . The groups most likely to conduct such operations include al-Qa'ida and the Sunni extremists that support their goals against the United States. These groups have both the intentions and the desire to develop some of the cyberskills necessary to forge an effective cyber attack modus operandi . . . Aleph, formerly known as Aum Shinrikyo, is the terrorist group that places the highest level of importance on developing cyber skills. These could be applied to cyber attacks against the U.S.[28]

Understanding the True and Full Scope of Vulnerabilities

We know from all of the cyber attacks committed over the past decade and a half that our networks are vulnerable to numerous types of assaults. We also know that intruders can penetrate networks and, once inside, steal information, alter information, or otherwise disrupt the functioning of the network. "Denial of service" attacks can impede network functionality as well as cause the loss of crucial business operations, and different types of malicious code such as viruses and worms can spread around the world in a matter of hours, if not minutes, and disrupt numerous networks indiscriminately. These examples clearly indicate that networks are vulnerable to attack, that businesses and Government operations can be disrupted, and that Internet traffic can be substantially impeded.

What is not known, however, is the full extent of harm that could be caused by the most sophisticated potential adversaries. For example, how much concrete economic damage could a sophisticated, well-planned, and well-coordinated cyber attack by a foreign nation do to the United States? Could the Internet as a whole be brought down and, if so, for how long? What effect could a significant cyber attack have on military command, control, and communications systems during peacetime or military conflict? These questions are all hotly debated, but as of yet, they have no clear answers.

Moreover, to say that computer networks are vulnerable does not mean that the critical infrastructures—such as electrical power grids, air traffic control, financial services, and gas and oil pipelines—that rely on those networks are necessarily vulnerable to significant disruption or that a cyber attack on an infrastructure would have a sufficiently long-lasting, destructive effect to achieve a terrorist's or nation-state's military or political objectives.[29] We still do not know the full extent of our critical infrastructures' vulnerabilities to various types of cyber attacks and the extent of cyber attacks' potential effect. But we should not wait for a major infrastructure attack to occur before we take steps to learn the full scope of our vulnerability and to begin shoring up our weaknesses. A major effort is needed now to fully assess the scope of our vulnerabilities before our adversaries demonstrate them for us.

The State of U.S. Countermeasures: Detection, Investigation, and Prevention

Our ability to withstand and effectively respond to major cyber attacks that could affect our national security depends on several categories of activity—some by Government, some by the private sector, and some by both. At the tactical level, we must be able to detect an adversary's preparation for or launch of a cyber attack early enough to take steps to defeat it or to contain damage. Currently, detection is dependent, in large part, on the reporting by private companies and Government agencies to the NIPC, to industry Information Sharing and Analysis Centers, or to computer security organizations such as the CERT/CC at Carnegie Mellon University or the Federal Computer Incident Response Capability (FedCIRC). With few exceptions (such as for the financial services industry, which must report "suspicious activity," including network breaches, to regulatory agencies), this kind of reporting is completely voluntary. And although reporting has certainly increased in the last 5 years (as indicated by the NIPC's and FBI's growing caseload of cyber attack investigations), the general consensus is that the vast majority of computer security incidents are not reported to any entity. Moreover, the proliferation of different private sector Information Sharing and Analysis Centers (ISACs) and continued interagency rivalries have prevented the sort of aggregation and analysis of incident data that is necessary to determine whether an attack is imminent or under way, where it is coming from, and what the effects are on a national level. The consolidation of various Government cybersecurity entities (such as parts of the NIPC, the Critical Infrastructure Assurance Office, the FedCIRC, and the National Communications System) in the Department of Homeland Security should, in theory at least, ameliorate some of these problems and improve the Government's ability, first, to aggregate and analyze data, and then, to discern indicators of a national-level attack and issue appropriate warnings so protective action can be taken.[30] However, as long as voluntary reporting by human beings remains the principal means of obtaining data about network attacks, information will, at best, be incomplete and late in coming. Our ability to detect, analyze, warn of, and thwart or contain the effects of attacks will therefore remain deficient. A crucial area for study, therefore, is how to construct a regime—through technology, law, or both—that yields more information faster and thereby improves our ability to detect and respond to a major cyber attack while protecting individual privacy rights and not unduly burdening industry.

A second area of activity crucial to effective response to cyber attacks is investigation and attribution of the source of an attack. Determining who is responsible for an attack is crucial to deciding what our response should be. If Solar Sunrise had been the work of the Iraqi military, for instance, then the U.S. response surely would have been different from what did occur (which was prosecution of the two California juveniles). But unless and until sufficient information is gathered to determine an attack's source, the Government's response is effectively hamstrung. Imagine the consequences, for example, if DOD had launched some sort of automated destructive counterattack (a "hack-back," as advocates of the action called it at the time) against the source of the Solar Sunrise intrusions as soon as the intrusions were discovered. The counterattack not only would have been highly embarrassing when it was discovered that the targets were American teens but also could very well have led to a criminal prosecution of military personnel for violation of the Federal Computer Fraud and Abuse Act.

At present, our ability to investigate and determine the source of an attack depends largely on two sets of activity: (a) investigation by law enforcement (or, where the legal predicate exists, foreign counterintelligence) authorities within the United States and in conjunction with foreign law enforcement agencies abroad and (b) intelligence gathering by intelligence agencies outside our borders. Law enforcement has the lead responsibility within our borders because all that the Government typically knows in the hours or days after a network attack is that a crime has occurred. Only after information is gathered can the Government determine that an intrusion is not only a crime but also either an act of espionage by a foreign intelligence agency or the precursor to an information warfare campaign by a foreign military. However, relying on law enforcement methods to gather information—which can involve getting court orders, serving subpoenas, interviewing witnesses, and the like—can take considerable time. Although such a delay may not pose major problems when the intrusion is a simple criminal event, it could cause enormous problems in the event of a true information warfare campaign or a cyberterrorism attack. In that case, considerable damage could occur before enough information is known about either the attack or the attacker to be able to respond effectively. With respect to our intelligence activity abroad, pinpointing the source of a cyber attack—or even identifying the true point of origin as opposed to a "hop site"—is no easy technological matter. Thus, another major area of study is how to facilitate faster investigation of cyber attacks and attribution of their source in ways that are consistent with civil liberties.

Finally, perhaps the most important area of "countermeasures" involves prevention—making our computer networks less vulnerable to attack in the first place. Presently, our approach to prevention consists of attempting to patch specific vulnerabilities in inherently insecure networks as those vulnerabilities become known. But new patches come out so frequently that implementing them quickly and effectively (while making sure the patches do not themselves cause a problem on the network) can be, for administrators of large networks, at best an extremely difficult job. We have seen cyber attacks again and again exploit vulnerabilities that were known for months, if not years, and for which patches were available but that not all system administrators had been able or willing to fix.[31] Clearly, we must move from this "Band-Aid" strategy to a world in which systems are more inherently secure and in which Government agencies and companies consider security to be a higher priority.

The question is how to motivate both manufacturers and users of computer hardware and software to take security more seriously. To date, the Government has relied almost entirely on a "soapbox strategy": warning of the urgency of the problem, urging manufacturers to make more secure products, and cajoling network owners and operators to devote more attention to their own cybersecurity.[32] Both the Clinton and Bush administrations have consistently rejected the notion of regulating vendors or users.[33] Although the Government has not dismissed completely the notion of creating market incentives to enhance security, it has not actively encouraged those types of measures either.[34]

Although good arguments can be made against direct Government intervention in this fast-moving, high-tech area, the evidence seems clear after more than 5 years that the "soapbox strategy" is not sufficient. Vulnerabilities in software persist.[35] Attacks continue to increase. And the possibility of a significant attack by a sophisticated adversary—whether a nation-state or a terrorist group—remains and, in fact, is growing as existing and potential future adversaries develop cyber attack capabilities.[36] Clearly, more is needed to secure our systems against attack. But what?

During the course of 2002, the Institute for Information Infrastructure Protection (I3P) hosted a series of workshops with software and hardware manufacturers, researchers, corporate users, infrastructure operators, and Government officials to gather input for a national cybersecurity research and development (R & D) agenda. During those workshops, which were focused largely on technical requirements and technology R & D priorities, experts from all of the communities repeatedly stressed the need for changes in the legal, policy, and economic environments to foster cybersecurity. Without these kinds of changes, these experts asserted, advances in technical R & D would never suffice because there would not be an adequate market for new security technologies. Based on this input, the final I3P agenda (released on January 30, 2003) identifies as a top research priority the study of various options for achieving legal, political, and economic environments more conducive to security.[37]

At the very least, research is needed to understand better the risks and economic costs that stem from cyber insecurity. Corporate executives and Government officials lack a solid understanding of the true nature of the risk to their enterprises, including the potential costs of various types of attacks and of the costs and benefits of varying levels of security they could put into effect. Cost-benefit calculations are therefore extremely difficult and often forsaken altogether.

Beyond providing cost-benefit analysis, we need a better understanding of potential mechanisms that Federal and State Governments could use to improve the state of security. Direct regulation is, of course, one possibility. And indeed, some regulation is already occurring, though in limited or indirect ways. In the Health Insurance Portability and Accountability Act[38] and the Gramm-Leach-Bliley Act,[39] for example, Congress imposed on health care providers and financial services firms, respectively, general requirements to take steps to ensure the security of their electronic systems. In addition, the Federal Trade Commission (FTC) brought unfair trading practice actions against—and reached settlements with—Microsoft and Eli Lilly, claiming that both had misled consumers by not having in place security measures sufficient to live up to their promises about the security and privacy of customer information. Both settlements required the companies to institute security measures, and the FTC's actions can be viewed as setting de facto security standards for companies that handle consumer information.[40] Finally, a new California law (effective July 1, 2003) requires entities conducting business in California to disclose computer security breaches if the breaches result in unauthorized access to California residents' unencrypted personal information (such as account, credit card, driver's license, or social security numbers).[41] The law also provides for a civil damage action by injured customers against businesses that violate the new law. This law is likely to have broad national effect in light of the number of companies that "conduct business" in California.[42] These varying approaches can be seen as experiments in regulation that might have broader applicability. At the very least, study is required to determine their efficacy in improving security and their costs.

Study also should be given to "softer" approaches designed to foster greater security without direct imposition of security requirements by the Government. These approaches might include the following: tax incentives to increase network security expenditures; legislation to create or enhance liability on the part of manufacturers or network operators for negligent actions or omissions that harm others; insurance requirements or incentives for security investments; requirements for public companies to discuss potential cyber risks or actual security breaches in their annual Form 10-K disclosure to encourage CEO and Board attention to security (similar to the approach used by the SEC to address Y2K concerns); and general standards or best practices for hardware and software manufacturers or certain critical industries.[43] Rather than simply dismiss out of hand these types of approaches—which are commonplace in other areas—we should acquire a solid understanding of their pros and cons and then pursue the best options.

Conclusion

As the one country in world history that is most dependent on information technology, the United States remains uniquely vulnerable to cyber attacks that could disrupt our economy or undermine our security. Although past attacks have largely been the work of individual hackers, protest groups, or criminals seeking illicit financial gain, cyber attacks also pose a threat to national security. Cyber espionage has been occurring since the 1980s and probably happens today far more than the Government even knows. Terrorist groups appear to be increasingly interested in using computers not only as communication devices but also as weapons to attack critical infrastructures. And information warfare is likely to be a part of every significant military conflict involving the United States in the future. To fight and win tomorrow's wars, we must prepare now (a) by improving our ability to detect, investigate, and respond to cyber attacks and (b) by exploring more effective ways to foster greater security of networks so they are less vulnerable to attack.

Notes

[1] The *2002 CSI/FBI Computer Crime and Security Survey*, conducted by the Computer Security Institute with the FBI (Spring 2002), reported all-time highs in the percentage of respondents who detected system penetration from the outside, "denial of service" attacks, employee abuse of Internet access privileges, and computer viruses; the survey can be accessed at http://www.gocsi.com/press/20020407.html. In addition, Riptech, Inc.'s July 2002, *Internet Security Threat Report, vol. II*, stated that, for the 6-month period starting January 1, 2002, Internet-based attacks increased 28 percent over the previous 6 months, contributing to a projected annual growth rate of 64 percent; see http://enterprisesecurity.symantec.com/content.cfm?articleid=1539&PID=12807550&EID=0.

[2] Bradley Graham, "Bush Orders Guidelines for Cyber-Warfare," *Washington Post*, February 7, 2003, http://www.washingtonpost.com/wp-dyn/articles/A38110-2003Feb6.html.

[3] Dorothy E. Denning, *Information Warfare and Security* (Reading, Mass.: Addison-Wesley, 1999), 73; David Ronfeldt, John Arquilla, Graham E. Fuller, and Melissa Fuller, *The Zapatista Social Netwar in Mexico* (Santa Monica, Calif.: RAND, 1998).

[4] NIPC, "Major Investigations: Mafia Boy," available at http://www.nipc.gov/investigations/mafiaboy.htm.

[5] David McGuire and Brian Krebs, "Attack on Internet Called Largest Ever," *Washington Post*, October 22, 2002, http://www.washingtonpost.com/wp-dyn/articles/A828-2002Oct22.html.

[6] In January 2003, for example, the "SQL Slammer" or "Sapphire" worm, which exploited a previously identified vulnerability in Microsoft's SQL Server 2000, quickly spread around the globe and adversely affected tens of thousands of computers. It reportedly disrupted some bank ATM machines, the electronic reservations system of a major airline, the Web sites of several financial services firms, and operations of emergency 911 systems outside Seattle, Washington. See SANS Institute, "A Special Report From the SANS Research Office: MS-SQL Server Worm (also called Sapphire, SQL Slammer, SQL Hell)," available at http://www.sans.org/alerts/mssql.php; Brian Krebs, "Internet Worm Hits Airline, Banks," *Washington Post*, January 26, 2003, http://www.washingtonpost.com/wp-dyn/articles/A46928-2003Jan26.html; "Internet Worm Keeps Striking," CBSNEWS.com, January 28, 2003, available at http://www.cbsnews.com/stories/2003/01/28/tech/main538200.shtml.

[7] Elinor Mills Abreu, "FBI Probing Theft of 8 Million Credit Card Numbers," *Reuters Internet Report*, February 19, 2003 Andrea L. Foster, "Computer-Crime Incidents at 2 California Colleges Tied to Investigation into Russian Mafia," *Chronicle of Higher Education*, June 24, 2002,available at http://chronicle.com/free/2002/06/2002062401t.htm; U.S. Department of Justice, "Press Release: Russian Computer Hacker Convicted by Jury," October 10, 2001, available at http://www.usdoj.gov/criminal/cybercrime/gorshkovconvict.htm; National Infrastructure Protection Center, "Major Investigations: Bloomberg," available at http://www.nipc.gov/investigations/bloomberg.htm.

[8] Senate Armed Services Committee, Subcommittee on Emerging Threats and Capabilities, *National Infrastructure Protection Center*, March 2000, http://www.fbi.gov/congress/congress00/vatis030100.htm.

[9] Toshi Yoshihara, *Chinese Information Warfare: A Phantom Menace or Emerging Threat*, (Carlisle, PA.: Strategic Studies Institute, November 2001), 3–5, available at http://www.iwar.org.uk/iwar/resources/china/iw/chininfo.pdf.

[10] Testimony of Director of Central Intelligence George Tenet, Senate Select Committee on Government Affairs, June 24, 1998, available at http://www.cia.gov/cia/public_affairs/speeches/archives/1998/dci_testimony_062498.html.

[11] English-language translation of Qiao Liang and Wang Xiangsui, *Unrestricted Warfare* (Beijing, China: PLA Literature and Arts Publishing House, Beijing, China, February 1999), available at http://www.terrorism.com/documents/unrestricted.pdf.

[12] iDEFENSE, Inc., white paper, "Inside the China Eagle Hacker Union," April 29, 2002, available at http://www.idefense.com/papers.html.

[13] John Arquilla and David Ronfeldt, eds., *In Athena's Camp: Preparing for Conflict in the Information Age* (Santa Monica, CA: RAND, 1997).

[14] Institute for Security Technology Studies, *Cyber Attacks During the War on Terrorism: A Predictive Analysis* (p. 13), available at http://www.ists.dartmouth.edu/ISTS/counterterrorism/cyber_attacks.htm.

[15] House Committee on Government Affairs, Subcommittee on Government Management, Information, and Technology, July 26, 2000, available at http://www.fbi.gov/congress/congress00/vatis072600.htm.

[16] Clifford Stoll, *The Cuckoo's Egg* (New York: Pocket Books, 1989); Denning, *Information Warfare and Security*, 205–206.

[17] House Committee on Energy and Commerce Subcommittee on Oversight and Investigations, testimony of National Infrastructure Protection Center Director Ronald Dick, April 5, 2001, available at http://energycommerce.house.gov/107/hearings/04052001Hearing153/Dick228print.htm

[18] Senate Armed Services Committee, Subcommittee on Emerging Threats and Capabilities, testimony of Michael Vatis, March 1, 2000, available at http://www.fbi.gov/congress/congress00/vatis030100.htm.

[19] Dorothy E. Denning, "Is Cyber Terror Next?" (New York, NY: Social Science Research Council, November 2001), available at http://www.ssrc.org/sept11/essays/denning.htm.

[20] Senate Select Committee on Intelligence, (testimony of Federal Bureau of Investigation Director Louis Freeh), May 10, 2001, available at http://www.fbi.gov/congress/congress01/freeh051001.htm.

[21] Denning, *Information Warfare and Security*, 68.

[22] Ian Bruce, "Al Qaeda Using Internet in Bid to Regroup," *The Herald* (Glasgow), March 7, 2002, p. 10, available at http://www.theherald.co.uk/news/archive/7-3-19102-0-52-33.html.

[23] Denning, *Information Warfare and Security*, 69.

[24] Canadian Security Intelligence Service Counter-Terrorism: Backgrounder Series, no. 8 (Canadian Security Intelligence Service, August 9, 2002), available at http://www.csis-scrs.gc.ca/eng/backgrnd/back8_e.html.

[25] Office of Critical Infrastructure Protection and Emergency Preparedness, Government of Canada, *Threat Analysis: Al-Qaida Cyber Capability*, December 20, 2001), available at http://www.ocipep-bpiepc.gc.ca/opsprods/other/TA01-001_E.asp.

[26] Barton Gellman, "Cyber-Attacks by Al Qaeda Feared," *Washington Post*, June 27, 2002, http://www.washingtonpost.com/ac2/wp-dyn/A50765-2002Jun26.

[27] Ibid.

[28] Senate Select Committee on Intelligence, *Worldwide Threat* hearing (CIA's "Questions for the Record"), February 6, 2002, available at http://www.fas.org/irp/congress/2002_hr/020602cia.html. (The CIA filed its written responses on April 8, 2002.)

[29] James Lewis, "Assessing the Risks of Cyber Terrorism, Cyber War, and Other Cyber Threats" (Washington, D.C.: Center for Strategic and International Studies, December 2002), available at http://www.csis.org/tech/0211_lewis.pdf.

[30] "Department of Homeland Security Reorganization Plan" (November 25, 2002), available at http://www.whitehouse.gov/news/releases/2002/11/reorganization_plan.pdf.

[31] A recent example of this trend involved the SQL Slammer worm. See note 7, above.

[32] Sarah Scalet, "They Want YOU for a Safer Infrastructure," *CIO Magazine*, June 15, 2002, available at http://www.cio.com/archive/061502/safer_content.html.

[33] The Clinton administration's *National Plan for Information Systems Protection* stated that "the President and Congress ... cannot and should not dictate solutions for private sector systems" (available at http://www.ciao.gov/publicaffairs/np1final.pdf). The Bush Administration's *National Strategy to Secure Cyberspace*, released on February 14, 2003, similarly states that "federal regulation

will not become a primary means of securing cyberspace" and that "the market itself is expected to provide the major impetus to improve cybersecurity" (p. 15, available at http://www.whitehouse.gov/pcipb/policy_and_principles.pdf). See also Molly M. Peterson, "Public-Private Partnerships Called Key to Cybersecurity," March 12, 2002, available at http://www.govexec.com/dailyfed/0302/031202td2.htm; Robin Weisman, "Bush Administration Talks Up IT Security," *Newsfactor Network*, May 16, 2001, available at http://www.newsfactor.com/perl/story/9788.html; James Middleton, "U.S. Cyber Terrorism Plan 'Flawed,'" *VNU Net*, 17 May 2001, available at http://www.vnunet.com/News/1121741.

[34] Art Jahnke, "Clarke Says No Tax Credits for Cybersecurity Measures," *CIO Magazine*, 16 October 2002, available at http://www.cio.com/research/security/edit/101602_clarke.html.

[35] Popular mailing lists such as the NIPC's "CyberNotes," <www.nipc.gov>, and SecurityFocus Online's "BugTraq," <online.securityfocus.com/archive/1>, continue to post dozens of new vulnerabilities every week.

[36] Statement of Lawrence K. Gershwin, National Intelligence Officer for Science and Technology, "Cyber Threat Trends and U.S. Network Security," before the Joint Economic Committee, June 21, 2001, http://www.cia.gov/cia/public_affairs/speeches/archives/2001/gershwin_speech_06222001.html; , "Cyber Attacks During the War on Terrorism: A Predictive Analysis," Sept. 22, 2001, available at http://www.ists.dartmouth.edu/ISTS/counterterrorism/cyber_attacks.htm.

[37] The I3P R & D agenda can be found at http://www.thei3p.org/documents/2003_Cyber_Security_RD_Agenda.pdf.

[38] Health Insurance Portability and Accountability Act of 1996, Pub. L. no. 104-191, § 1173, 110 Stat. 1936. Available at http://frwebgate.access.gpo.gov/cgi-bin/getdoc.cgi?dbname=104_cong_public_laws&docid=f:publ191.104. The Department of Health and Human Services published in the Federal Register the final rule implementing the security provisions of HIPAA on February 20, 2003. The final rule can be found at http://www.cms.hhs.gov/regulations/hipaa/cms0003-5/0049f-econ-ofr-2-12-03.pdf.

[39] Gramm-Leach-Bliley Financial Services Modernization Act, Pub. L. no. 106-102, 113 Stat. 1338 (1999). Available at http://www.senate.gov/~banking/conf/confrpt.htm.

[40] Barbara Yuill, "FTC Approach in Recent Settlements Creates Information Security Road Map," *BNA's Privacy & Security Law Report* 1 (33): (August 19, 2002).

[41] California Senate Bill 1386, available at http://info.sen.ca.gov/pub/01-02/bill/sen/sb_1351-1400/sb_1386_bill_20020926_chaptered.html.

[42] Alex Salkever, "Computer Break-Ins: Your Right to Know," *BusinessWeek Online*, Nov. 11, 2002, available at http://www.businessweek.com/technology/content/nov2002/tc20021111_2402.htm; Kevin Poulsen, "California Disclosure Law Has National Reach," *Security Focus Online*, Jan. 6, 2002, available at http://online.securityfocus.com/news/1984. Moreover, Senator Diane Feinstein is reportedly considering introducing similar legislation in the U.S. Senate (See Patrick Thibodeau, "California Leads Way on ID Theft Legislation," *Computerworld*, Dec. 13, 2002, available at http://www.computerworld.com/securitytopics/security/privacy/story/0,10801,76721,00.html.

[43] SEC Staff Legal Bulletin no. 5, Jan. 12, 1998, available at http://www.sec.gov/interps/legal/slbcf5.htm.

Chapter 8

Enhancing Cyber Security for the Warfighter

Sean R. Finnegan

A key element of current and future U.S. warfighter capabilities is and will be the information systems being integrated into almost every aspect of military missions. This integration of computer systems will continue, driving new capabilities and efficiencies as well as creating increasing potential for damage from attacks by adversaries on information systems.

To date, the United States has been fortunate; significant cyber-attacks have not been mounted against operational Department of Defense (DOD) systems, but the potential clearly exists. Although the media and general population are focused on worms, viruses, and hackers who are motivated primarily by the desire for peer recognition or to cause trouble, these visible and public attacks are, in most cases, rather unsophisticated. The more serious threat to DOD comes from more determined adversaries with extensive resources and the desire to compromise these information systems silently, disrupting warfighting capability by waiting for the moment of greatest effect.

Until very recently, cyberattacks have followed a clear cycle that starts when a vulnerability is found and reported to the product vendor. The vendor then fixes the problem and makes a patch available to customers. Weeks or, more often, months after the patch is available, an exploit code to attack systems with this vulnerability is created and, in the most destructive cases, this exploit is wrapped in worm or virus code. The use of these exploits in self-propagating code is typically indiscriminate, and the effects are often very obvious (e.g., Web site defacing).

This cycle gives the user (or administrator) an extensive period of time in which to update his or her systems. Unfortunately, experience has shown that many systems both inside and outside of DOD are not updated, even months after the patch is available, leaving them vulnerable to attack.

To make matters worse, this cycle, with its delays and flaws, is really the best-case scenario for DOD to protect its systems.

A more serious prospect involves DOD systems facing a dedicated cyberattack from an adversary using an exploit previously unknown to the vendor or DOD and for which no patch is immediately available. A serious adversary might make every attempt to conceal the attack and the subsequent compromise of DOD systems until he has attacked a sufficient mass of systems to further disrupt critical DOD capabilities. This "zero day" attack using stealth and a previously unknown exploit likely will occur, and the current DOD focus on border protections will be ineffective because the attacker will already be inside the protected enclave. Any effort to mitigate this threat will take a combination of vendor and DOD efforts. Vendors need to work toward producing more secure software, and DOD must deploy systems to detect and react to new vulnerabilities and threats.

Band-Aid or Preventive Medicine?

Many observers refer to the current approach of preventing vulnerabilities as a "Band-Aid" strategy whereby vendors simply issue patches in response to a vulnerability rather than attempt to create more inherently secure systems. Although this impression is not uncommon, it fails to recognize the enormity of the challenge that vendors face and the actions they have been taking to improve the overall security of their products.

Over the past few years, the high-tech industry has witnessed an incredible shift in the threat environment in which their products must operate. Although systems were once stand alone or networked in small, isolated networks, the expansion of the Internet and the increasing interconnectivity of even closed networks has resulted in an environment where adversaries could launch distributed attacks from anywhere in the world and mask their true identity by routing these attacks through unwitting hosts. Not too long ago, only small groups of highly skilled professionals, typically within national defense establishments, knew how to analyze and exploit the security of information systems. The skill set required to attack information systems was obscure and the techniques closely guarded. Today, however, these skills are widely known, and an entire cottage industry has grown up where individuals seek out and publish vulnerabilities in vendor products to gain public notoriety.

Vendors now find themselves racing to locate and address security vulnerabilities before they are found externally, yet, for decades, no significant advances have been made in developing more secure systems. Computer programming remains a human process and, as such, is very error prone. Reviving fundamental research in ways not only to make programming less error prone but also to create systems that are self-repairing and self-maintaining is critical. These types of advances are likely a decade or more away. In the near term, vendors such as Microsoft are engaging in efforts to improve the security of the code they produce through developer education, advanced code scanning tools, process improvements, and advances in testing. These efforts are known within Microsoft as the Secure Windows Initiative and, despite the name, involve all product groups within Microsoft. The following sections describe these activities in greater detail and serve as a representative example of the efforts being put forth by industry to counter an increased and increasing cyber security threat.

Education

Microsoft and all other software vendors compete for developer resources from the same pool of industry professionals and college graduates. In the vast majority of cases, these developers have received no formal training on secure development practices, including use of threat modeling in design, ways to avoid common coding errors like buffer overruns, and proper applications of security features such as encryption or user authentication. To address this problem, Microsoft has developed its own internal curriculum for training developers on secure coding practices. It requires that all developers, testers, and program managers complete this training and also makes the training available on demand by means of online video. The course curriculum has been published as a commercially available book, and the same course is offered to third-party developers through their authorized training center partners.

For other security measures, Microsoft has updated the documentation provided to outside developers to include security considerations for relevant Application Programming Interface calls. Additional education activities include working with universities to develop security curricula in computer science programs so future classes will graduate into the industry already having the needed skills.

Process Improvements

In addition to educating developers on secure coding practices, Microsoft also has made improvements to its internal development processes. For example, product functional specifications now include a "Security Considerations" section to ensure that security is considered at the beginning of the development process and that progress against mitigating these risks is checked at key milestones in the development cycle. One of the keys to making these security considerations effective is the proper application of threat modeling and risk assessment to the product plans. The Secure Windows Initiative team has developed its own methodologies for this application based on its experiences within Microsoft and its work with the development teams to create threat models and determine appropriate counters to threats based on risk.

Steps also are being taken to reduce the functionality that might be available in default installations and that an attacker might target in all new products—known as the "attack surface" of the product. Where, once, Microsoft shipped products with all functionality turned on to make it easy for users to discover, new product versions ship with unnecessary functionality disabled. In addition, fundamental design changes are being made to run product features with lesser privileges so even a successful attack will have limited effect. These efforts will result in DOD product users needing to apply fewer patches because only minimal functionality will be installed and available for attack.

Unfortunately, Microsoft can take these measures only with new products and cannot change the default configurations for shipping products. For current shipping products, Microsoft produces tools to automate the securing of existing installations, and it works with centers of excellence in the security community such as National Security Agency, Defense Information Systems Agency, National Institute of Standards and Technology, and others to develop security guidance that must be applied to DOD systems.

Tools

One of the most effective ways to reduce vulnerabilities in software is through the use of advanced tools that can scan through source code and locate potential problems. Microsoft has been investing in these types of tools, and the most effective of these is known internally as PREfix. The PREfix tool not only scans source syntax for potential problems based on a canonicalization of similar issues but also emulates the execution of specific segments of code in memory to test conditions that would be difficult or impossible to test with traditional "black box" methods. However, these tools are far from a panacea and must be tuned so they do not produce too many false positives and thus encourage developer complacency. These tools also must be trained for specific types of problems, and in

Microsoft's case, it is using input from previous security vulnerabilities to train these tools.

Finally, a number of compiler vendors have started adding technology to compilers that will attempt to mitigate the risk from stack-based buffer overruns that could lead to system compromise. The new technology involves placing code on the stack so, if the code is overwritten by an attempted exploit, the program will terminate rather than allow the exploit to occur. This approach is effective at mitigating some classes of buffer overruns, but it does not prevent all attacks and is not a replacement for solid coding practices.

Testing

One common perception is that security vulnerabilities are a result of vendors failing to test their products thoroughly before shipping. This assertion has some merit in that many systems now in use by DOD were designed and released long before the highly interconnected threat environment of today. Poor assumptions may have been made by the developer that an attacker would not create his or her own "client" application to attack a system or that attacks would come by means of applications that behaved in expected ways. Of course, we know this assumption is no longer valid, and vendors have had to strengthen their testing practices appropriately.

In Microsoft's case, the company has supported over the past several years extensive development of stress-testing tools designed to attack exposed system interfaces and thus find potential vulnerabilities before a product ships. Coupled with the threat models and risk analysis being performed, this approach has resulted in current-generation products that are significantly more secure and resilient to attack. In addition, many vendors are supporting government security evaluation programs such as the Common Criteria (CC) and 140 evaluations. Microsoft, Oracle, Sun, and others have submitted their products for evaluation under CC, and the result is clearly more secure products. However, these evaluations do not produce perfect products, and the process can be very expensive and time consuming. In the case of the Microsoft Windows 2000 evaluation, this effort took nearly 3 years and, by the time the evaluation was complete, the company had released a newer version of the operating system. Despite the time lag, the company and customer still benefited from the evaluation because what was learned during the Windows 2000 evaluation was rolled into Windows XP before release.

Fortunately, DOD has recognized the problem caused by waiting for completion of a Common Criteria evaluation before allowing the use of a product and has clarified its policy to permit the use of products while they are being evaluated. However, this policy change has done little to increase the rate of new technology adoption in DOD. A challenge for both industry and DOD is support for preexisting or legacy platforms and the slow speed of technology adoption. DOD is like many large customers in that adoption of new technology often takes years of planning, testing, and evaluation before deployment even begins. Even then, deployment can be painfully slow. The result is an environment in which DOD not only is unable to take advantage of new functionality in new products but also is not able to benefit from advances vendors have made in creating more secure products.

Compounding this problem is the fact that older products often cannot be secured to the same degree as newer ones. Older products may use legacy protocols with known weaknesses and, to maintain compatibility with the older products, vendors also must include weaker protocols in the newer products. DOD needs to study ways to more rapidly adopt newer products to remove the risk introduced by legacy products and protocols.

People, Process, and Technology

DOD has long had a difficult time hiring and retaining enough people to manage its information systems effectively and securely. In deployed scenarios, the situation is exacerbated because systems administrators often have very little experience, and they add another logistical requirement to the warfighting force. As the number of systems continues to increase, this situation will worsen, and all large enterprises will need to adopt more automated systems to manage the security of their Information Technology infrastructure. The days of having enough system administrators to follow elaborate procedures to secure a system and physically touch each machine requiring an update have long since passed.

DOD needs to accelerate the deployment of management infrastructures for information systems through which small numbers of security experts will be able to define and automatically deploy security configurations appropriate for the current threat environment. Along with the deployment of management systems, more focus should be placed on upgrading existing legacy platforms to newer products that are more easily managed and that are designed to work within the new frameworks.

The real benefit of these management infrastructures is not only that they will help make DOD information systems "secure" but also that they will allow information security managers to make systems "secure enough" for the environment. In most other security disciplines—such as physical security—DOD long ago recognized that the organization could not afford to stay at the highest security level at all times. Maintaining computer and information systems at the highest state of security costs time and money and can lead to complacency. In addition, the information security needs will vary with the particular environment in which the system is working. For example, the security posture of a system needs to change as it is moved from a base to deployment in the field where the possibility of capture or compromise is heightened.

With automated security management systems, DOD could start performing actions such as requiring rapid password resets or disabling the use of certain weak legacy protocols as the "INFOTHREATCON" level increased. Much like the color-coded Homeland Security alert levels, automated security management systems could alert users to be extra vigilant to potentially dangerous cyber activities, and additional resources could be deployed to monitor intrusion detection systems when needed.

Unfortunately, the culture of DOD makes implementing these kinds of systems very difficult to do. The vast majority of DOD information systems are procured, configured, and deployed at the individual base or component level. The organization demonstrates great reluctance to allow centralized deployment of security patches and configurations for fear that it might adversely affect a mission-critical application. Although these concerns are certainly valid, a number of steps can be taken to reduce the risk of adverse effects:

- Identifying and maintaining a list of systems or applications that are truly mission critical—where any interruption would have a grave effect on mission capability—and that allow security management infrastructure to treat these differently
- Testing systems against the security posture for each threat level to clearly understand the effect of increased security levels
- Ensuring the capability to roll back the immediate deployment of security patches for systems that experience failures (which will require support from the product vendor to realize)

In the end, though, DOD may have to accept these risks as being less risky than a cyberattack that uses a known weakness in the system. DOD should begin by working with procurement channels to ensure that all systems shipped are configured in a secure fashion and with some automatic update capability enabled by default. This default security posture will make it easier to maintain the security of systems that may not ordinarily be well managed but also will allow local components with their own systems management staffs to disable or modify this security to meet local needs.

Finally, although DOD faces a clear imperative to have a security management infrastructure, it is also important to note that these very management systems will likely become a focal point for attack by adversaries. For example, in Microsoft Windows environments, the Active Directory Group Policy infrastructure provides the ability to manage security settings for large numbers of machines by defining those security settings in the directory itself. These settings can be delegated hierarchically so component administrators can tailor the settings to their particular environment. However, if an attacker can gain physical or administrator access to the directory service where these security settings are stored, then the attacker could compromise the security posture of a large number of machines. Protection against this vulnerability must be factored into the design of any security management system, much as it is factored into the deployment and use of crypto systems.

The Pursuit of Perfection

Before deploying any new technology, DOD traditionally spends an extensive period of time designing and testing these systems. Systems often are not deployed or even considered unless they can solve all potential problems. This engineering approach means that desperately needed systems may take many years to evaluate, engineer, and deploy—and, in many cases, are already outdated by the time they reach the field.

DOD rapidly needs to adopt available technology for managing security patches, even if it may not have reached its end state. For example, enabling administrators to perform simple, in-place upgrades by managing 20 machines centrally rather than each one individually will significantly improve their ability to secure the infrastructure. Instead, the typical approach is to spend years engineering and designing a system that can manage thousands of machines while, in the interim, the security posture does not improve.

A widespread belief holds that no solution to improving security should be fielded unless it works for all platforms or applications. Again, this approach is, in principal, a good one, but such an idealistic requirement often results in a failure to adopt intermediate solutions that may improve the security posture of specific applications or platforms.

Defense in Depth

For the past several years, one of the cornerstone concepts in the defense of DOD systems has been the concept of "defense in depth." The general notion behind defense in depth is that systems should be designed with multiple layers of security such that a failure in one of these systems does not result in a successful attack because other layers will mitigate the risk. This approach is a good strategy with which most security experts agree, but in DOD and many other environments, its execution could be improved.

Current DOD efforts to carry out defense in depth rely heavily on one or more firewalls to provide a defense at the network layer, and then some level of host-secure configuration is provided. What is missing is a focus on providing multiple layers of defense within each individual host. For example, on the Microsoft Internet Information Server Web server platform, many DOD users will configure the Web server product securely and place a firewall in front of it. However, additional measures such as using IPSec filtering and higher level HTTP request filters on the Web server (such as URLScan), can be used to block potentially malicious attacks even if an attacker finds a new or "unpatched" vulnerability in the Operating System or Web server. On workstation machines, using personal firewall software that opens ports only in response to client outbound traffic or using products that, according to behavior, block malicious code could also provide additional layers of defense.

In general, the effectiveness of border-level protections in DOD networks appears to be decreasing steadily. The fact that the staff that administers the firewalls is often disjointed from personnel who administer and develop the applications has led to a firewall "arms race" in which application developers increasingly are funneling more and more network traffic over commonly open network ports (such as port 80 used for HTTP). Furthermore, we must anticipate that an attacker already has compromised at least one machine inside the network to establish a jumping off point before being detected. Once inside the network, any attempts to block the attack from the outside will be largely ineffective.

Again, using technologies such as IPSec, DOD could define machine-to-machine authenticated and encrypted communities of interest to help insulate specific mission systems in the event of an attack. This strategy includes the ability to define and change these secure networks in rapid response to changing threat environments and operational needs. Reducing levels of access when appropriate and rapidly restoring access when the threat has passed are key responses. Without the ability to both implement and remove these security measures quickly, people will be unwilling to use them when they are most needed.

Conclusion

The U.S. Department of Defense is relying increasingly on computer information systems to support warfighting capabilities and support its goal of network centric warfare. To accomplish this goal successfully, the systems deployed need to be secure enough to prevent an adversary from disrupting them and thereby reducing combat effectiveness. Fortunately, industry is following a similar developmental path by which software is becoming increasingly more secure to respond to increased threats present in all lines of business that are now heavily networked.

However, despite commercial attention, many challenges remain for both DOD and industry. Vendors must continue to focus on creating products that are secure in design, in deployment, and by default. Fundamental long-term research to improve the error prone nature of software development and to make systems that are self-securing and self-repairing should be conducted. DOD rapidly needs to put in place management systems and processes to better use their security expertise in systems management. Finally, DOD needs to avail itself of new technology as vendors provide more secure systems. Only through partnership with industry will DOD be able to deploy and maintain the type of networked warfighter systems ultimately needed.

Chapter 9

Complexity of Network Centric Warfare

Stanley B. Alterman

The U.S. Department of Defense is now committed to a transformational path toward network centric warfare (NCW) that is focused on combining, fusing, and collaboratively sharing data from a multitude of diverse intelligence gathering sensors. The effort will require a system-level architecture that presents a single, unified picture of the battlefield by accurately and dynamically compensating for time latencies and other physics anomalies inherent in this kind of integration. A wideband communications network will enable precision attack of valid, time-sensitive targets in real-time by the best available attack weapons systems. This chapter summarizes aspects of NCW as reported in unclassified interviews, military and commercial periodicals, and presentations by government officials and military leaders. Its intent is to look at network capability and to understand and minimize not only the complexities inherent in modern, IT-based networks but also their potential negative impacts.

To achieve the objective of NCW—enhancing the speed and reliability of command—all-source sensor information will be "posted within the network-available database before processing" to allow the collaboration and self-synchronization needed in flexible targeting. We must avoid undue focus on the sensors. Our objective will be the plug-and-play of current and future sensors into our open-architecture network. The high-speed solution to improved real-time targeting lies in the network architecture design. Present sensors will feed the network at first, and upgrades will come later, as long as the architecture is published with standards that are open. This approach is an ideal opportunity to use the "spiral development process," an incremental development approach that features trial and test procedures before advancing to higher performance levels.

Given the increasing complexity, mobility, and dispersion of air defense networks and critical, time-sensitive ballistic missile launchers;

WMD-related targets; key command centers; and expanding counterterrorist operations, it appears DOD must adopt the posture that is described in a recent *Aviation Week & Space Technology* article on NCW as "it takes a Network to beat a Network." In essence, we will be mimicking just-in-time manufacturing processes widely adopted by U.S. industry from succesful Japanese production methods to achieve military tactical efficiency and speed. However, we run the risk of sacrificing operational reserves by over-streamlining the network and reducing the normal redundancy and built-in inefficiencies if we don't intentionally allocate these reserves up front. As it evolves, this transformational concept assuredly will run up against organizational and operational complexities and will require compromises to make it work properly. To that end, DOD is opening the Transformational Communications Office (TCO), a small organization whose mission will be to coordinate, synchronize, and direct the execution of a transformational communications architecture. In short, the TCO will attempt to minimize the chaos of this evolving, complex architecture of network centric warfare. This process may be simplified if one recognizes that five existing grids of communications must interface and interoperate: satellites, theater, tactical, munitions, and surface. Each of these separate grids will have to conform to overall architecture standards.

Retired Navy Vice Admiral Arthur Cebrowski, who now heads the Pentagon's Office of Force Transformation, has earned the title "Father of Network Centric Warfare." He describes future requirements of NCW in the following terms:

> We are less concerned with the combat capability of expensive weapons platforms than their ability to function on a networked, information-age battlefield. This has to do with a weapons system information processing power . . . its command, control, communications, computer and intelligence, surveillance and reconnaissance (C4ISR) capabilities.

Cebrowski calls the portion of assets dedicated to C4ISR the "C4ISR fraction." The larger that fraction, the better the weapon system is suited to a network centric environment. He gives high marks to the Stryker, Joint Strike Fighter, Comanche, and the Navy's littoral ship concept because they all have invested in a large percentage of C4ISR assets that can interface with current and future user networks.

Today's primary sensors include the following: RC–135 Rivet Joint for signals intelligence; E–3 Advanced Warning and Control System for airborne target tracking radar and electronic support measures; E–8 Joint-Standoff Targeting Radar System (JSTARS), ground surveillance radar; Army Guardrail for communications intelligence; Royal Air Force Nimrod; U.S. Air Force distributed Common Ground Station; U–2; Global Hawk; EP–3; and Army Airborne Common Sensor A/C and space-based sensors. In the future, this network of sensors and communications will include the next generation 767-based Multisensor Command and Control A/C, which eventually will operate as part of the U.S. Air Force Multisensor Command and Control Constellation and the Battle Management Command and Control (BMC2) system. We also should expect to find the seamless integration and merging of advanced systems from all the military services into this common Integrated Information Infrastructure (III).

The Army's Future Combat System has the opportunity to provide "up close and personal" and continuous sensor data posted into this network as new, gap-filler, and authenticating sources. An increasing use of "incidental recce," or information derived from weapons themselves, can be expected from real-time bomb damage assessment; "throw away or leave behind recce" (reminiscent of, but massively superior to, the McNamara Line in Viet Nam); Stryker mobile vehicles; and the Army Digital Battlefield infrastructure.[1] The Navy's Cooperative Engagement Capability (CEC) has an important role in force protection and target attack assessment.[2] Unfortunately, because it is designed as a stovepipe system in itself, it requires upgrading to be a useful part of the network vision.

Promising advanced systems such as DARPA's network centric Affordable Moving Surface Target Engagement (AMSTE) program must be included in this open architecture network.[3] New, long-range, high-definition, airborne, multifunction, active, electronically scanned array radars (to be carried on E–8; Joint STARS later, on the Global Hawk Unmanned Vehicle System [UVS]; and, potentially, on B–2 and B–1) and a variety of other platforms are at the heart of the AMSTE concept. Coherent, multiple-aircraft triangulation against moving targets promises adequate accuracy for direct control of GPS precision weapons through the Joint BMC2 command and control network. Equally important will be multiple-platform (manned and UVS), passive, real-time, networked, hyperbolic triangulation systems (such as DARPA's Advance Tactical Targeting Technology) that can locate radiating targets with adequate accuracies for direct targeting or, at least, precision sensor queuing.

However, lest we fall into the fire of complexity of integrated networks while jumping out of the pan of stovepipe systems, we need to determine what drives complexity and apply the keep-it-simple-stupid principle inherent in stovepipe designs while also introducing the myriad advantages promised by network centric operations. What must be perfectly clear, however, is that network centric is not an array of stovepipe, single-service systems that can be made "network ready" to interface with a central network. The Services seem to have picked up on the need to use "network" in their marketing descriptions for new products and systems, but an examination of developments hyped in this way, for example, the Army's Ground Moving Target Indication (GMTI) sensors—which definitely are not joint—reveal a reluctance to embrace the core principles that define NCW. Lip service to a network mandate is not enough.

Many seem to think that OSD wants nothing more than proposals to integrate former and future proposed heterogeneous platforms and sensors into a common network. That, however, is not the NCW vision. The true NCW vision spelled out by John Stenbit's OSD command, control, communications, and intelligence (C3I) team is to "only handle information once," by posting information (any information in data format) to a ubiquitous and robust global information grid (GIG) network from which people on the network "edges" can pull the information they need when they need it (assuming it exists). One of the biggest hurdles with this vision is dispelling the issue of information "ownership" to allow those with proper access immediate access. One must recognize that substantive information differences will exist between "video" types of sensor data and electronic intelligence (ELINT) or communications intelligence (COMINT) digitized data, a subtlety that will have to be incorporated in the NCW architecture.

All agree that reconnaissance assets are the high ground of the future battlefield and that one military service branch trying to own that information for its own use is not possible. However, managing these sensor assets for everyone's use as eyes, ears, and even collectors is a subtle change in doctrine. We must clarify the concept of "sensor responsibility, integrity, and test." When an aircraft publishes a communications message onto Link 16, for example, that aircraft must be certified to publish.[4] If, in a similar fashion, that certification requirement is added to sensor data, this requirement will alleviate the quality control of the network and reduce the overall complexity of the NCW problem. The notion of sensor data integrity is a change to the concept of stand-alone sensors.

"Smart push," a concept that promotes forcing appropriate data to an end user, is also in the NCW vision, but by far the majority of information is dynamic and real time insofar as its existence (life cycle) on the network. The concept of "user pull," whereby users take information they require directly from the network, was to have been demonstrated in an advanced capability technology demonstration (ACTD) called Network Centric Collaborative Targeting (NCCT), where several USAF sensor platforms were to be linked or networked with the DCGS-USAF all together in a near-real-time sensor grid. To emphasize the "user pull" issue, shooter-to-sensor terminology was used in lieu of sensor-to-shooter. Unfortunately, although approved by the Assistant Secretary of Defense for Command, Control, Communications, and Intelligence and the Undersecretary of Defense for Acquisition, Technology, and Logistics, the Air Force could not fund the project from its budget. NCCT would be a good opportunity to formalize the NCW concept and architecture with a plug-and-play demonstration.

The term Web centric might be more useful than network centric to depict the type of architecture and the scope of changes involved in the new warfare doctrine. For example, Predator will post its data stream or sensor stream to a network node, which will allow this real-time, dynamic information to be posted on a URL-defined Web site. The relevant IP address will then be loaded into a user's thin client device when the user has determined that this particular Web site provides value-added information to support the user's activity. Web addresses for a variety of sensor data must be established. We should all keep in mind that "It's the architecture, stupid," and that the Internet architecture was formalized before the development of modems, servers, and all the equipment used to access the Internet.

Complexity of the Web centric vision is driven primarily by several issues, starting with the inherent size and complexity of the network, the speed and accuracy with which it must operate to succeed in its mission, and the redundancy and security it must have to achieve mission success. Issues like data ownership must be dispelled, and the need for smart push of critical data to specific users must be addressed. If successful, modern military networks can achieve decision superiority over their adversaries. We can get inside our adversaries' observe–orient–decide–act (OODA) loop. This is accomplished by the modern network's ability to process continuous observations while operating in real time with super precision, approaching near-zero-time actions/weapons engagement. These skills may well be critical on the modern battlefield where success may be achieved by catching and reacting to fleeting transmissions, all in a matter of microseconds.

A particularly stressing challenge in modern warfare is the attack of moving or moveable targets, particularly in dense, high collateral damage environments. The November 2002 successful "snapshot" kill of al Qaeda operatives in an automobile in Yemen demonstrates the power and desirability of achieving these kinds of successes. During the new mission, called Deadly Persistence, a loitering, hunter-killer Predator Unmanned Vehicle Ship (UVS), a predecessor of our future UCAV fleet, launched a remotely targeted Hellfire missile and struck the automobile and its occupants with minimal damage to nearby objects.[5] In a major tactical scenario, larger numbers of moving targets (with diverse sensor data and weapons available in the battlefield) would amplify the difficulty and complexity of achieving this type of mission success.

The Hellfire used in the recent Predator operation is an infrared imaging weapon. Ultimately, to achieve the same successes, we will have to launch GPS weapons (our battlefield precision weapon of affordability and choice) such as Joint Defense Air Munitions (JDAM), a 2,000-pound GPS precision bomb; its newer, future relative, the Small Diameter Bomb (SDB); and even smaller, more precise future weapons. The SDB will have only a 250-pound yield warhead and, thus, will require more precision in real time to allow update of a moving target GPS position. These updates will require some form of real-time data link for target update as part of real-time network tracking data. There is much discussion of how to obtain an affordable data link to each smart bomb and how to devise a way to receive visual feedback results just before impact of each bomb or weapon, along with Bomb Damage Assessment by subsequent, re-targetable weapons carrying appropriate imaging sensors.

These communications concepts vary from taking advantage of the existing data channel capacity on GPS NAVSTAR satellites and using the installed GPS receiver to receive target updates (a solution not without international spectrum and political ramifications), to using existing, more expensive data links such as Joint Tactical Information Distribution System (JTIDS) or Common Data Link (CDL), to future plans for a Joint Tactical Radio System(JTRS) communications systems. These real-time targeting demands are inherent in the notion of network centric warfare and will increase as we move closer to that vision and further away from classical "platform centric" thinking. Although targeting is the primary issue, if we have very good blue force (friendly forces) location and maneuver data, Admiral Cebrowski reports, we will not necessarily avoid killing the innocent, but the ambiguity of friendly fire will be removed from the equation. This issue likely will have a major effect on coalition warfighting. The British are struggling with their own version of a "network-enabled strategy." The necessity of international coalition integration and warfighting raises fundamental questions of network political oversight management, the need for more complex security, and operational rules of engagement. We must be wary of loss of sustained high-tempo operations and rapidly spiraling network centric development due to international political decision making.

Several additional complexities are inherent in network centric thinking. The necessity for faster "time to decide" systems and high-speed, real-time operations (including the necessary countermeasures to adversary avoidance) will require increased machine-to-machine interfaces coupled with advanced decision aids, which will increasingly cut human operations out of the decision loop. The NCW concept thereby preempts the normal chain of command operating in series within the decision loop by pushing down the decision process to lower levels of operational management, including automated decision aids. The radical nature of this type of design has caused discomfort in many DOD circles. Some officials and military lean toward maintaining the "artistry" of highly experienced intelligence analysts for "data ownership" and General Officer or Senior Staff for "decision ownership." Others contend that only the development of machine-to-machine connectivity will allow intelligence gathering to keep pace with a foe's ability to hide and disguise communications. In principal, our military and technological superiority would allow unfettered implementation of the NCW process, given appropriate attitude adjustment of senior officers.

The transition to NCW has other potential landmines in its path, many of which are unpredictable as we introduce new technology more quickly than we have done in the past. Complex networks will generate interdependencies, making risk assessment and protection difficult at best. The role of real-time network oversight by the command structure takes on comparable significance to operational, tactical command and control.

John Stenbit of OSD's C3I and now Assistant Secretary of Defense for the Networks and Information Integration office envisions the path toward the required communications network (referred to as the GIG or, alternatively, the III) with primary objectives that include the following:

- Increase the speed of decisions
- Increase the speed of attack
- Increase the speed of assessment (notwithstanding the special problems in assessing the effects of information operations)

In the C3I vision, people throughout the trusted, dependable, and ubiquitous network, empowered by their ability to access information and recognized for the inputs they provide, will enable real-time operations in precision warfare. Its mission is to lead the information age transformation of DOD by building a foundation for network centric operations through policies, program oversight, resource allocation, and value-added support.

The C3I goals are as follows

1) Make information available on a dependable and trusted network.
   - Achieve a ubiquitous, secure, and robust network
   - Eliminate limitations of bandwidth, frequency, and computing capability
   - Deploy collaboration capabilities and other performance support tools
   - Secure and assure the network and the information

2) Populate the network with new, dynamic sources of information to defeat an enemy.
   - Populate the network with all data (intelligence, nonintelligence, raw, and processed)
   - Continuously refresh network content
   - Consider all users of the information as suppliers—"post before process"
   - Improve "sense making" (i.e., put information out in a form that makes sense to the user)
   - Develop new ways to gain access to adversaries' information
   - Continuously surprise the enemy with the information we are using

3) Deny the enemy comparable advantages and exploit their weaknesses.
   - Effectively conduct offensive Information Operations (I/O)
   - Implement full-spectrum security
   - Conduct aggressive counterintelligence
   - Collect information with persistence, unconventionally, without warning, and unexpectedly

The C3I implementation philosophy:

- Promote revolution by means of transformational concepts

- Execute all the assigned tasks but allow latitude for less-than-perfect performance on some of them
- Address every issue from three perspectives: policy, programs, and resources
- Trust, integration, and collaboration are the rules
- Lead by example

Three example areas of "emerging opportunities":

- Software tools for collaboration within wide area networks; software "agents" to assist in collaboration
- New methods for determining network robustness; auditing tools that operate in real time and alarm rather than track; training and education
- New wireless technologies to address the "last tactical mile" challenges; cross-linking in space (laser and RF [EHF]).

Other related NCW thoughts and terms:

1) "task, process, exploit, and disseminate" (TPED) is being replaced as a warfighting strategy by "task, post, process, and use." (TPPU). This re-adjustment is trying to accomplish two needs:
   - Getting information to urgent users without going through processing (post before process)
   - Getting critical information to users without going through "ownership" paths (Smart Push)
2) C3I is rewriting the spelled out DII/COE standards to list only bare minimum requirements.
3) OSD has undertaken a C4ISR Transformation study to determine which of the myriad developmental programs they have
   - are transformational (continue those)
   - could be transformational (alter those)
   - are not transformational (cancel those)

Even though future adversaries may be less technical, unfortunately, we have leveled the playing field by our naiveté in commercial off-the-shelf (COTS) warfare, namely, our belief that, in disrupting the commercial communications and sensor information available to adversaries, we will maintain our own unfettered access. The availability of COTS capability to unsophisticated adversaries adds a new dimension to our network centric challenge. Commercial cell and space phones, precision location by means of GPS, and a future Galileo, night vision and space-based imagery level the battlefield and are available to all. According to John Arquilla and David Ronfeldt in "Networks and Netwars," a RAND research study, "terrorists can be expected to make use of all types of communications in innovative ways." Lt Gen Michael Hayden, director of the National Security Agency (NSA) said, "Terrorist communications are riding on the wave of a $3 trillion telecom industry and taking advantage of a system that's global, instantaneous, complex, and encrypted. NSA has to cope with key terrorist messages hiding in 160 billion minutes of international long-distance calls a year." This gap allows adversaries, including terrorist organizations, to "operate in a network-centric fashion using our communications networks."[6]

Perhaps six countries and some private companies have sensor satellites that, while not as good as those used by the United States, are able to supply solid intelligence, count tanks, track fleets, and acquire useful military movement information. In a recent interview, according to former CIA Director George Tenet, "Foreign military, intelligence, and terrorist organizations are exploiting this commercial capability to enhance the planning and conduct of their operations." However, U.S. military satellites remain the best because they can discern far more detail and collect more images. To maintain our superiority, a new generation of collection satellites, part of a project called "Future Imagery Architecture" (FIA), is planned.

Our own increased use of commercial and dual-use systems provides interesting new vulnerabilities. Of particular concern is our increasing reliance on navigation, location, and timing from systems like GPS to operate in a dynamic environment. Network centric warfare is based on "where you are and what time it is," in the words of trained operators, and GPS accuracy is critical to this effort. Reducing errors from 40 feet to 10 feet in target locations enables direct target attack with precision GPS weapons. GPS is the core asset required for NCW to work. However, a recent report from the National Training Center advises of "the proliferation of GPS jammers—small, effective, and inexpensive jammers that will block GPS signals eliminating GPS navigation and precision guidance capabilities within an extensive area of operations." The report further urges, "we learn—or re-learn—how to either fight without GPS capability or more importantly fix the problem of GPS vulnerability."

As we learned at a substantial cost in Iraq, it is essential that we fix the GPS vulnerability problem immediately and re-think the chain of command structure. Fixing the GPS vulnerability problem is relatively easy with available user equipment anti-jam technology and requires not much more than the dedication to do so. Although money always will be an issue, in the long run, doing nothing will be more catastrophic and costly. As far as organization is concerned, a possible solution is to restructure military thinking similar to the current U.S. Navy fleet model where the Admiral in charge of the battlegroup "rules by negation," and the fighting element commander (ship Captain) is the real-time decisionmaker with suitable reduced levels of information reported above. The Admiral thus provides "guidance," not real-time command and control.

As the decision process gets pushed down to lower and lower levels in the network, real-time "precision complexity" is reduced. Military networks consciously can be designed to have multiple levels of interaction loops with different performance demanded in each network loop. The senior commanders' roles then change from real-time operation to general guidance and error detection and correction, which unburdens the network and adds an oversight function, minimizing errors. Undoubtedly, once the network is "complexity minimized," residual vulnerabilities will remain because of reliability, interference, jamming, etc., but a simpler network with continuous oversight will be far easier to keep functionally operational.

A digital-versus-analog overlay issue is yet another element of the network vulnerability problem. Our current use and reliance on conventional, clocked, synchronous, miniature logic circuits adds new vulnerabilities. For example, at .25-micron feature sizes, radiation hardening of microchips may be required at all altitudes rather than only in space. We are moving toward intentional use of High Power Microwave (HPM) and Ultra Wideband (UWB) as disrupting signals, and, in some cases, as operational signals in the battle space. Our own clocked logic processors are equally vulnerable to this type of intentional or unintentional disruption. Additionally, most military (and commercial) communications rely on getting time synchronization and location data from a vulnerable GPS satellite constellation.

A related challenge is the "fuzzing" of spectrum allocations, allowing higher levels of interference between now well-defined spectral boundaries. The FCC allowance of UWB spectrum operation is only the most recent example, spilling over many important spectrum areas, including GPS and commercial communications allocations. Our thinking must change to the use of asynchronous, "clockless" processing to minimize electromagnetic interference (EMI) effects as well to preclude "eavesdropping" and EMI vulnerabilities in the complex digital battlefield.

Complexity is further amplified in the Information Operations (I/O) environment of future battlefields. The USAF, as reported in a recent *Aviation Week* article, is trying to get its arms around this enormous problem—and potential—with the following concepts and perspectives. The RC–35 Rivet Joint fleet, the EC–130 Compass Call fleet, and the AF 55th Wing, including Cobra Ball and Combat Scent intelligence gathering aircraft, are part of the 8th Air Force, now referred to as the Information Operations Combat Force. The 8th AF has cells of intelligence officers embedded in Space Command to allow total sensor integration. Their reports state, "It is hoped that an appropriate offensive counter computer algorithm can strike in seconds when needed in consort with hard weapon attack in the NCW arena." This goal is a good start, but not without problems. The following insights are from AF I/O planners as presented in a recent Electronic Warfare (EW) conference, but they are equally representative of all the military services' thinking process:

1) The USAF is trying to move from the potential impact of I/O in warfare (enormous) to the capability to impact (lacking).
   - Need is to get an offensive EW capability
   - Plan is "Information Attack 2010," which will include electronic attack, electronic protection, and EW support.
2) Measuring the effect of I/O is very difficult.
   - How do you measure the "cognitive effect" on the enemy?
   - Need modeling and simulation as well as data that provide effectiveness results from exercises, red teaming, etc.
3) USAF is re-looking its organization, trying to determine how to present I/O to the warfighting commanders, especially in light of
   - Merger of U.S. Strategic Command and U.S. Space Command
   - DPG emphasis on I/O (14 studies mandated)
4) Trying to resource I/O is difficult.
   - The amount of money spent on I/O and Information Warfare (I/W) is unknown.
   - There is no I/W Capability Requirements Document (CRD) or Program Decision Memo (PMD).
   - There are serious Program Object Memo (POM) problems.
   - Acquisition cannot keep up with the technology cycle.

5) USAF is looking at whether they should have I/W as a separate career path.
   - Select officers from intel, communications, space, and flying fields.
   - Put officers in an I/W "track" with a career management plan.
   - Consider that, with all the services reaching for solutions in I/O, our own complex, networked systems will probably be the most vulnerable to I/O attack.

So, where are we? As we move from stovepipes to networks, we introduce various complexities, including organizational, operational, and technical, with new and subtle vulnerabilities that are attributed to the expanded use of more automated processes. We have an opportunity at the outset to minimize these inherent complexities by design, not with after-the-fact patches.

Recognizing the criticality of the issue, SECDEF suggests three options to move forward:

- Create a separate agency to develop and deploy a network centric BMC2 system.
- Allocate money to all combatant commanders to buy "joint" BMC2 systems.
- Authorize and allocate monies to JFCOM to buy "joint" BMC2 systems.

All understand that NCW is not a new communications system, a faster computer, or a new platform or sensor. A recent *Aviation Week & Space Technology* article defines NCW as a unified concept of operations that is glued together with a "social structure of networking," "protocols," and "rules of interaction allowing multiple machines and users to collaborate and provide mutual support to one another." The challenge is to accomplish this monumental task while minimizing the complexity inherent in these types of real-time integrated networks with elaborate man-man, man-machine, and machine-machine interactions. The objective is to evolve a "plug-and-play" network with a "spiral development" transformational process. In this process, picking the correct starting point is critical.

Notes

[1] On February 27, 2002, the Army formally named its new Interim Armored Vehicle the "Stryker." The Stryker, the combat vehicle of choice for the Army's Interim Brigade Combat Teams (IBCTs), is a highly deployable, wheeled armored vehicle that combines firepower, battlefield mobility, survivability, and versatility with reduced logistics requirements.

[2] CEC provides enhanced warfighting capability to all participating ships and aircraft by fusing track measurements from air-defense sensors within a battle group into a single composite track—resulting in greatly improved track accuracy and continuity.

[3] The goal of the AMSTE program is to develop and demonstrate a new strike capability: the ability to target moving surface threats from long range and to rapidly engage those threats with precision, stand-off weapons.

[4] Link–16 is the new tactical digital information link (TADIL) now being implemented. It provides several significant improvements over existing TADILs: nodelessness, jam resistance, flexibility, increased security, increased number of participants, increased data capacity, navigation features, and voice.

[5] *Aviation Week & Space Technology*, November 11, 2002, 34.

[6] *Aviation Week & Space Technology*, November 16, 2002, 55.

Chapter 10

Difficulties with Network Centric Warfare

Charles Perrow

As network centric warfare (NCW) rapidly becomes the key innovative military posture in the United States, it may be useful to examine some problems it raises. The preceding chapter on the complexity of NCW serves as my text. While ultimately skeptical about the promise of NCW, Stanley Alterman takes us on a useful tour of the myriad groups, offices, and buzzwords swarming about this enterprise.

Swarming, as in the collective activity of birds and bees, is the latest idea being applied to business, industry, and the military. The notion is that agents with limited intelligence or none at all are guided by a small set of rules, such as staying close to other agents while avoiding obstacles and self-organizing en masse to reach a goal. This notion comes quickly to mind when reading accounts about DOD plans and weapons involved in the NCW effort. Alterman's discussion lists the acronyms for seven new or reconfigured units, infused with 21 programs, along with four demonstrations and studies used with 19 assets. The complexity of interactions envisioned in this example of NCW is startling. One can foresee the fog of war being replaced by the fog of systems.

Much of my work as an organizational theorist has been concerned with the unexpected dangers of complexity. It is a truism that complexity can lead to failures, and nearly as prevalent a truism that the interdependencies inherent in complexity are threatening. Certainly, the sprawl of multitudinous agencies, programs, and assets that Alterman describes demonstrate "interactive complexity" wherein the multiple errors—inevitable in themselves and, individually, of no great consequence—combine to defeat safety systems. If the system is also "tightly coupled," it will crash.[1]

Two alternatives for the face of future warfare are often presented—one, a fantasy, characteristic of the optimistic NCW literature and, the other, not so neat but more intriguing and potentially more realistic. The fantasy is the pages of bulleted Boy Scout homilies about the improved and increased speed of decision, attack, and assessment; the ability to establish trust and dependability; the advent of full-spectrum security, robustness, collaboration, dynamic sources of information, continuous information refreshment, battlefield sense-making, surprise, aggressive counter-intelligence, integration and collaboration, super precision, everything in real time and simplified; and so on. Although these terms and concepts are ubiquitous in the NCW literature, I do not think anyone believes these conditions really exist or that, in calling for them, they will come. However, pages of idealistic possibilities have been published by the Assistant Secretary of Defense for Command, Control, Communications, and Intelligence, by the Chief of Naval Operations, by military experts, and by others.

An equally enthusiastic report on NCW by *Aviation Week* also suggests caution.[2] Breathless with promise, the report cites only two empirical examples of the advances in NCW; one was real, the other a training evolution. In the real-world case, an F–14 that was out of munitions radioed a B–52 to use its munitions on the targets the F–14 had identified. Hardly much. The second situation, though only a training operation, was more impressive. Using the Joint Tactical Information Distribution System, all F–15s in a formation sent radar information to one another and to Airborne Warning and Control System (AWACS) aircraft, producing a composite radar picture. That example is nifty, but the question must be asked: Are there not more dramatic examples of actual use of NCW? Very possibly, more examples exist, but the only other mention of NCW I could find, which I will come to later, was a complete failure. Colonel John Rosenberger, Commander of the 11th Armored Cavalry Division, offers many detailed and alarming examples of the failure of Blue Teams, equipped with the latest NCW equipment and strategies, to defeat Red Teams who lacked them.

Skepticism about NCW shows up in Alterman's convincing warnings with respect to GPS vulnerability, the ability of enemies to exploit commercial information networks, and, particularly valuable, two separate dangers: stovepipes and micromanagement. Stovepipes result from the classic organizational difficulty in attempting to solve problems with innovative techniques. Ideally, to address a problem, one wants several independent, autonomous sources of experimentation rather than a single centralized one because, that way, a variety of schemes can be tried. Different organizations have different skills, and one skill is almost guaranteed to be more innovative than the others. The difficulty lies in the fact that individual systems will not have logical interdependency—the ability to communicate with one another—without which implementation on a systemwide basis is impossible.[3] In a perfect world, after all the experimentation is finished, the best plan—the one that best meets the needs of all users in all forces—is chosen. In practice, determining when experimentation should end and the final decision is good enough is difficult. The scrap rate is enormous; some users typically are dissatisfied with the final choice and surreptitiously retain their stovepipe system, not fully using the official chimney. Meanwhile, the final chimney, the most naturally efficient system, tends to be harder to modify or dismantle than the stovepipes when the situation changes and offers to adversaries a big, single target. Achieving interoperability of locally optimal systems is, at best, difficult.[4]

No neat solution to this classic problem in constructed systems is readily available. Systems that have made progress on this problem have done so through evolution and a variety of practices such as starting local and small, tolerating cost overruns and outright failures, trying to be just good enough rather than perfect, rotating personnel through diverse units rather than merging units, and never expecting or promising much. But these strategies are not without risk. Cobbling together a bricolage of stovepipes both degrades their local utility and increases the possibilities of unexpected interaction among errors. All attempts to standardize weapons for use by multiple services have encountered these problems. For this reason alone—the dilemma of local innovation and centralized hardening—the dreams of Admiral Cebrowski, considered by many to be the father of the NCW concept, and those of others likely will not be realized in the next couple of decades. Indeed, the volume of expectation and promise may have to be lowered. DOD has to pursue NCW because our enemies now possess the capabilities to damage stovepipes; however, the current push toward the swarming of organizations, tactics, and weapons, while intended to make us more effective, may be a counterproductive resort to technology, thus driving out the push for innovative strategy and tactics.[5]

The 1999 National Training Center (NTC) exercise in Alameda, California, offers a warning of the potential failure in an exclusively technology-driven push to NCW. During the exercise, Blue Team members were issued GPS-linked, handheld, real-time screens showing the deployment of the Red Team and allowing them to send information to correct the images. The devices, however, were too complex to use, even in simulated combat.

For a fraction of the cost of the GPS devices, the Red Team purchased a bunch of walkie-talkies of the kind used by longshoremen in the Oakland Port. With simple, short-range communications and a focus on innovative tactics to compensate for their primitive equipment, the Red Team defeated the Blue Team.[6] The failure speaks to the potential limitations of NCW as currently envisioned.

The second concern with respect to the current NCW layout is a classic problem in organizational theory: the ownership, volume, and credibility of information. Information management within the chain of command is the cornerstone of military operations worldwide. The standard bureaucratic structure, which has served us well, does not maximize information sharing; to maximize sharing invites the problems of micromanagement. The standard structure selects and summarizes information at each level of the bureaucracy rather than maximizes it. This approach reduces the workload of the next level. Perhaps more important, it protects the lower unit from unwise interference from above. I am told that successful communication in Naval battle groups required the squadron commander to find empty sites on the Internet where his sailors could communicate easily with instant messaging without fear of being monitored by higher authorities. Only that which is necessary for the higher level to know is passed up; otherwise, the higher level, not having the time or experience to evaluate what is going on at the shop floor, will give incorrect orders. The shop manager must be trusted to know what is best for workers. As a general rule, neither communications nor information should be maximized; they are expensive and can overload the system. The true art is deciding what not to communicate. I could find no musings about this approach in NCW literature, which seems to assume that all information should be communicated to all levels.

The bureaucratic structure of military and industrial organizations served our information needs well in the past. Because of the high cost of information and the unwieldy, limited channels (bandwidth, in Internet terms), information economy was forced on organizations. However, when the cost of information and communication dropped dramatically with the electronic revolution, information management then entered a new realm. Suddenly, a chief executive officer 10 stories and 10 levels above a data processor could count keystrokes, backspaces, and even order a dismissal. Micromanagement became not only easy but also almost expected. While the private sector has had many problems with this trend, the military seems to have had even more. Every advance in war fighting seems to have fostered micromanagement. NCW takes this trend to the extreme. To sever the elective affinity between NCW and micromanagement, we will need something far more robust than what is delicately described by Alterman as "appropriate attitude adjustment of senior officers." Information must be compressed and summarized at each level, which means more delegation of authority to compress and summarize. The genius of the bureaucratic form, used by all modern organizations, was delegation of authority, and with that came protection from information overload and reduced opportunities for micromanagement.

How do we handle the prospect of micromanagement in NCW, short of relying on "attitude adjustment"? Stovepipes reduce micromanagement but thwart interoperability. The answer may lie in "scale-free" systems, where units can be added without increasing hierarchy. Scale-free means that a distribution is not dominated by any representative scale. In conventional organizations, adding more units will increase the hierarchy because another unit must then be added to supervise and integrate the new units. The structure of a conventional organization resembles a bell curve; even if comparatively flat (decentralized), as it grows, it must swell in the middle. Scale-free systems need not. The Internet, for example, has a spike at one end of the distribution and an "outrageously long and heavy tail," indicating it can grow without thickening or raising the height of the spike (the "backbone").[7]

We have four current examples of social systems that are scale-free, adaptable, reliable, and either decentralized or vertically disintegrated. The first example is small networks of firms such as high tech industries in northern Italy and the Silicon Valley electronics industry and biotechnology industry in the United States. The second example is the three national power grids: the Eastern Interconnected System, the Western Interconnected System, and the Texas Interconnected System. The Internet is a third example. The fourth example, alas, is terrorist networks. NCW aspires to be a fifth type of scale-free system.

Consider the centric in network centric. In an ideal NCW structure, centric refers to the top tier, tier 1, which can have access to all information in the system if needed but which, in practice, relies only on summaries too brief to overload the tier. Tier 1 does not include generals and admirals in the usual sense but, rather, "coordinators" who look only for major imbalances and make adjustments. For example, in the networks of small firms, the top tier alerts marketing units and educational institutions about major shifts in technology and consumer preferences. In the power grids, tier 1 shifts power between major segments of the grid. Tier 2 enforce rules, after semi-autonomous units make allocative decisions in tiers 3 and 4. In the Internet, tier 1 concerns involve packet routings in the backbones, for example, when a major player like WorldCom or Sprint steps out of line and violates protocol. Tier 1 in the terrorist network gives broad orders about financial flows, major targets and timing, and media activities. Tier 1 deals with only highly aggregated information processed by the lower tiers.

In all systems, tier 2 is spatially disaggregated. In the power grid, major population centers and clumps of rural areas are the basis of aggregation; in the Internet, the lead servers in geographical space constitute the backbone. Tier 2 is local coordination for the networks of small firms and for the terrorist cells. In the networks of small firms, tier 2 consolidates the work of tier 3 and 4 producers by product line and by technological processes. Sometimes, networks of small firms cluster about a major firm without being dependent subcontractors because other major firms also seek their output. Small-firm networks may not even have a permanent central coordinating level (the "centric" in network centric) but may rely, instead, on a variety of small distributors and marketers. If there is a central firm, it serves as a coordinator of the inputs from the two or three or four levels of subcontractors below it rather than from a central authority.

What all four examples have in common is radical decentralization wherein the lowest level units are, to some degree, self-organizing and, to a high degree, autonomous, that is, free from micromanagement. They achieve this state in quite different ways, none of which may be compatible with NCW but all of which are worth considering. The power grids are run by coordinating groups and financed by the utilities, but they operate independently of both. Below these coordinators are two or three levels of largely autonomous and often self-organizing controllers that balance loads. The Internet has policemen or traffic cops dispersed across the globe to intervene only in cases of persistent congestion or disruptions. Below them are servers and, below those, routers; each adjusts and learns without human intervention. The Internet is a vast organization that adds units daily without increasing the hierarchy and that functions without centralized control. The terrorist network has a short, primitive hierarchy with self-organizing and largely autonomous cells, which can increase in number without creating any need to reorganize the system.

All four systems are scale-free, adaptive, and resilient, and contain built-in redundancies. None would be successful if they were micromanaged, if they were to depend on one vulnerable source of information such as GPS, or if they were the product of a forced marriage of independent service cultures, each with its own chain of command. What would it take to move our military in the direction of these networked systems? The four systems all have differences, so drawing from the examples must be judicious.

The grid and the Internet rely on high tech processors, "intelligent agents" such as the routers, servers, and load adjusters, that learn from experience. Efforts to develop similar equipment for the military are under way. Yet, although room exists for intelligent agents, it would be folly to rely primarily on technology to wage future wars and conduct all future military operations. More relevant to the military are the firms and terrorist groups. Neither of these has intelligent agents. Instead, they rely on the small size of their "distributed agents," as we might call the firms and cells, with their flexibility, adaptability, and intense socialization. The military could replicate these types of structures; indeed, much of the rich military tradition revolves around these types of decentralized units.[8] Surely, this consideration deserves as much effort and attention as does the technology model.

Another critical aspect of scale-free systems is that, in all four of the current examples, networking grew gradually. The systems were not conceived in substantially full form and then put into effect from above; they evolved through trial and error in cultures that allowed change. In every case, the current culture locates leaders below the top. The top sets grand strategy, allocates resources, and coordinates; it does not lead in the usual, heroic military sense. That, anyway, is how it looks to an organizational theorist new to the topic of NCW.

The battlefields of Iraq, Afghanistan, and Bosnia hardly can be said to illustrate the power of NCW as characterized by the enthusiastic promises of its advocates. Instead, these engagements illustrate the power of control of the air, smart bombs, accurate targeting by artillery and tanks, and overwhelmingly superior numbers and fire power—and in the case of Iraq, a demoralized enemy not modernized in more than a decade. We cannot count on these conditions in future wars. Our incipient NCW plans may suffer defeat by either the equivalent of Colonel John Rosenberger's Red Team, using primitive but cagey techniques and being inspired by an ideology we can neither match nor understand, or by an enemy who can knock out our vulnerable GPS or use electromagnetic pulse weapons on a limited scale, thus removing intelligence as we have construed it and have come to depend on it. Fighting forces accustomed to relying on downlinks for information and commands would then have little to fall back on.

In NCW, shared, complete information is the key, and we are building our forces around it. But, the system is extremely vulnerable, so we should see how those forces perform when information is not shared and not complete. War games should be run with degraded communication and even erroneous information supplied by enemy hackers. Run the games with multiple friendly fire incidents that wipe out secure communication links and demoralize our troops. Remove unit commanders at each level down to the squads and see how the subordinates fill the gaps. Limit the topmost echelon to monitoring and communicating only in response to requests. Cut off supplies and see how the troops make do. Exercises of this kind would reveal the vulnerabilities of a system designed for a future war against a sophisticated and resolute enemy. These enemies exist.

Notes

[1] C. Perrow, *Normal Accidents: Living With High Risk Technologies* (Princeton, NJ: Princeton University Press, 1999).

[2] William Scott and David Hughes, "Nascent Net-Centric War Gains Pentagon Toehold," *Aviation Week & Space Technology*, January 27, 2003.

[3] Steven M. Rinaldi, James P. Peerenboom, and Terence K. Kelly, "Critical Infrastructure Interdependencies," *IEEE Control Systems Magazine*, December 2001.

[4] An example of a near-chimney that has limited the search for Internet security is Microsoft. Much of cyber-terrorism, so well described by Mike Vatis in chapter 7, might be traced to Microsoft's dominance, its inferior Windows system to which it clings, and its lack of concern, until recently, with security. The small stovepipes such as Linux that have sprung up cannot compete because the Microsoft chimney dominates software. For an interesting account of Linux, see <http://firstmonday.org/issues/issue5_3/kuwabara/index.html>.

[5] Milan Vego, "Net-Centric Is Not Decisive," *Naval Institute Proceedings*, January 2003.

[6] Joel Garreau, "Reboot Camp: As War Looms, Marines Test New Networks," *Washington Post*, March 24, 1999, C1.

[7] Steven Strogatz, *Sync: The Emerging Science of Spontaneous Order* (New York: Hyperion, 2003) and Duncan J. Duncan J. Watts, *Six Degrees: The Science of a Connected Age* (New York: W.W. Norton, 2003)..

[8] Reliability in the grid, Internet, and small firms is achieved through two forms of reliability: replication redundancy (or link redundancy) where the architecture of the structure is replicated in each unit, making it possible to have multiple links among peers, and mirror redundancy where the content rather than the structure is replicated. In essence, part of that which each unit knows is key information about the structure of all other units and the contents of messages each unit is sending. If failures occur, then—for example, in producing a part in the small firm or generating enough or too much energy in the grid or in coping with misrouted or damaged packets in the Internet—other units can produce the part or the energy, or replicate the lost packet. The terrorist network is vulnerable in this respect, and it differs from the others because security requires that units not share addresses and contents. Its reliability has to depend on a simpler and more expensive form of redundancy: replacement redundancy; if one cell is disabled, another must take its place.